Sailing On A Dream

Tyler Rush Bangert

authorHOUSE®

AuthorHouse™
1663 Liberty Drive, Suite 200
Bloomington, IN 47403
www.authorhouse.com
Phone: 1-800-839-8640

First published by AuthorHouse 12/12/2008

ISBN: 978-1-4389-1494-7 (sc)
ISBN: 978-1-4389-1495-4 (hc)

Library of Congress Control Number: 2008910009

Printed in the United States of America
Bloomington, Indiana

This book is printed on acid-free paper.

Dedication

To my father, Richard Wallace Bangert,
who taught me how to embrace life,

and to my son, Richard Sonten Bangert,
to whom I hope to teach the same.

Chapter 1

Leaving Palau

I drifted up from a peaceful sleep, opening my eyes to dim light. The soft morning glow allowed me to see shapes, but not details. It was still early. The residue of a dream was still in my mind, but it was slipping fast. All I could glean from it was something involving Dad, and the feeling it left me with was pleasant.

I let go of these dream remnants as I threw off my sheet, and I got up. I was now fully awake and ready for the day, of which I had been waiting a long time. I climbed up the three steps from below and emerged on the deck of the *Suena* – the sailboat I was on.

It was a beautiful morning! We were anchored in a protected cove, surrounded on all sides by the Rock Islands. The sky was cloudless and blue, yet it still had that morning quality. It was slightly cool, which invigorated me. The air was fresh and had a familiar smell – the ocean, the saltwater, the reef and the humid smell of tropical jungle vegetation. The familiar smell was comforting, and I was reminded of the time I first experienced these smells six years earlier when I first arrived at these islands. Yet the knowledge that these smells would soon no longer be a daily occurrence heightened my awareness, making the smells seem strangely foreign.

There was a slight breeze that caressed my face and added a whisper to the morning as it blew through the nearby trees. There were a number of birds singing already, and I could hear the gentle lap of water against the hull rocking the sailboat ever so slightly.

The *Suena* was thirty-six feet long, and was classified as a sloop or cutter. Apparently there is no accepted distinction between the two. It had one mast and three sails: the main sail attached to the rear of the mast and the large boom that usually hung to one side of the cockpit, the jib was the foremost sail attached to the mast and the bow, and the staysail – the smallest sail – was between the jib and mainsail. As we were anchored in this protected cove, the main sail was reefed, and the other two were furled. As I looked at these sails I could hardly believe I was standing on the deck of a sailboat – an ocean worthy sailboat – and about to embark on a journey of 1500 miles. I was about to fulfill a long held dream.

It seemed appropriate, almost providential, that "Suena" means Dream.

The cove we were anchored in was amongst the Rock Islands of the Republic of Palau. We were surrounded on all sides – except for a very narrow passage to the east – by the limestone uplifts that were the Rock Islands of Palau. The surrounding islands rose sharply 500 to 600 feet above the water and were thick with jungle vegetation. The limestone of the island was made of compacted coral reefs, which were the skeletal remains of marine organisms. These islands represented millions of years of life in the making and billions of organisms. The life – both present and past – was mind-boggling in its abundance and beauty.

The sun was up by this time, but the *Suena* was still in the shadow of the Rock Islands. The islands were carpeted in lush local vegetation: pandanus, hibiscus, plumaria, tangang-tangang, various vines, and countless other types of foliage. Birds soared above the tops of the highest trees, played tag among the hanging vines, skimmed the calm surface of the water, or called to each other as they headed out to sea to fish for the day. The water in the cove ranged from pastel green to spiritual blue, with every hue of blue and green in between. The water itself was like glass that reflected a shimmering double of the Rock Islands above. The breeze, almost imperceptible, stirred the water and slowly turned the sailboat, giving me a panorama view of the surrounding beauty.

I stood there in awe, giving myself a last chance to let this beauty to soak into my being, for I knew I would be leaving that paradise that very day, possibly to never return. I could also feel the excitement running through my veins; my dream I had shared with Dad from the time I was a young teen to sail the ocean blue was about to become reality. In fact it had; I had already spent my first night on the *Suena*. Unfortunately Dad wasn't with me; he had died fourteen years earlier.

My excitement for the imminent journey, however, was also mingled with apprehension. Could I – a complete novice and landlubber – learn all that was needed to help sail a boat from Koror, Palau to Darwin, Australia? Raise and lower sails? Adjust sails? Read a compass, use a Global Positioning System (GPS) and keep the boat on course during my watches? Keep night watch and the *Suena* safe? Tie nautical knots? Plus all the other thousands of essential details and adjustments that needed to be made on an open ocean sailing journey (not to mention get along with two people on a thirty-six foot boat, people I had only meet days before)? I had never sailed on a sailboat before – even on a lake. Had I gotten myself in water too deep?

These concerns and apprehensions, however, only seemed to add to the excitement of my impending adventure.

My sister and I had often wondered if Dad still watched over us, even though he had been dead for so many years. She firmly believed he was present during an unpleasant custody battle years earlier. I couldn't dispute what she said, and I had wondered if he was present that day in the post office. I had been in the Koror post office only weeks before when a notice on the wall caught my eye. I usually don't pay attention to the clutter on the Post Office bulletin board, but this time my intuition – or something – told me to look. The plain, unassuming notice read, "Wanted – One person to crew on a sailboat to Australia." To me it seemed to say, "Your dream continues here!"

When I was a teenager, Dad and I had dreamed of buying a sailboat and sailing the world. In fact, with a friend of Dad's we even began to take lessons that would eventually result in a license to navigate harbors. Dad and his friend began to look for a sailboat to buy. It was an exciting time: taking lessons, looking at pictures of sailboats we might buy, dreaming with Dad. I was even going to take a year off from high school to sail. The fact that we lived in Colorado, far from any ocean, did not deter us. We were going to actually do it.

Then Dad got sick, and in less than a year he was dead. The dream was off. At least for the time being.

When this opportunity to fulfill the dream Dad and I had together presented itself I couldn't pass it up. I was on the phone within the hour. A few days later I was on the *Suena* introducing myself to Rick (the captain) and Phyllis (his companion).

Rick was of medium build and height, and had short sandy hair, and a close cropped well trimmed beard and mustache. His grey eyes seemed to express a certain playfulness, but there was also something guarded there, although I knew not what. It was similar to the feeling of seeing a dog wagging its tail for you, yet something told you it was capable of biting with the wrong movement.

Phyllis was a thin woman, about five and a half feet tall, dirty blond hair that fell below her shoulders. She was of average looks, but she had a sincere smile that showed her own positive outlook on life and added a sense of confidence to the atmosphere. Both Rick and Phyllis were in their late thirties or early forties.

We sat in the cockpit at the stern of the *Suena*, in the shade of a large canopy erected over the rear of the sailboat. We talked as the *Suena* slowly turned this way and that according to the direction of the light breezes. Already I was falling in love with this gentle motion and the relaxed atmosphere.

I was honest about my lack of sailing experience – none, in fact – but my enthusiasm and attitude helped to balance that. For me everything almost seemed too perfect: the timing was right (they were setting sail just after my school year ended); Rick and Phyllis seemed like easy people to be with and our conversation was natural and flowing; I had always wanted to go to Australia; but mostly, I had always wanted to realize the dream Dad and I had to sail the open deep blue sea. All the right conditions were lined up!

My only hesitation at that time was that I was anxious to get home after being away for so long. Ten days to two more weeks seemed like along time, and I was concerned how I would handle the cramped conditions. But I knew I would never forgive myself if I passed up this opportunity; I was sure ten days would go quickly and even two weeks would be bearable, and anyway, Rick gave the impression that even two weeks was a conservative estimate.

Before I left, Rick and Phyllis expressed interest in me, but they wanted time to make a final decision because they had interviewed some others and had one or two more to see. They gave me a simple book about sailing to study while I waited for them to call me back with their decision.

Over the next weeks I was anxious to hear from Rick and Phyllis, and I was both excited to go yet scared they might actually decide on me. In the intervening time I studied the sailing book and I managed to see the movie, "Wind," about sailboat racing. Both increased my desire and hope, and added to my excitement. When the phone call finally came I was ready to go and the duration of ten days to two weeks ceased to be a concern.

I had arrived on Palau six years earlier on a two-year teaching contract. Obviously, I liked Palau as two years quickly became six, but it was time to leave. It would be hard to leave, but an exit by sailboat could at least be a balm to soothe the parting.

I wouldn't particularly call myself adventurous, especially when compared to people I have read about who really could be termed "adventurers." However, I wasn't a couch potato, either. I liked to live life and sometimes push the conventional trajectories a bit. After all, I was in Palau and not still in my home town, or home country; I had to travel about 10,000 miles to get to this "middle of the ocean" locale, live in a different culture, give up a lot of taken-for-granted everyday pleasures, such as fresh milk, driving on the highway, and twenty-four-hour electric and water service. But any loss of luxury I experienced was more than compensated by a wonderful experience in Palau. And although my entry permit said "Missionary" (because I had been teaching in a Catholic school), anything I offered was returned to me tenfold. Or more.

Palau is a small island nation in the west Pacific Ocean, southwest of Guam and east of the Philippines. During my time there Palau was the last Trust Territory of the

United States, yet frantically trying to become independent – but that's another story. There are approximately 200 islands in the Palau archipelago, eight of which inhabit a total of 15,000 to 17,000 citizens. Palau is most well known for its spectacular scuba diving and its beautiful Rock Islands, or, as they are sometimes called, the Floating Gardens. Being only seven degrees north of the equator, parts of Palau are the epitome of the stereotypical island paradise. However, with the influence of Japanese and Western cultures, Palau is no longer a pure island culture – but that, too, is another story.

I arrived in Palau six years earlier to teach at the mission, Mindszenty High School. I wanted to do something a little different, something other than just be another rat in the "rat race," so I joined the Jesuit Volunteers International (JVI). Similar to the Peace Corps in some ways, but the JVI had a strong spiritual component. Also, it was a fairly small organization which was, I believed, more personal. Also, the JVI only places its volunteers where there are Jesuits, of which I already had experience with. This made a new place already have something familiar to me, people I knew who could support me in my transition to a different culture, and who had similar beliefs. In some ways my motivation for joining the JVI was selfish. For instance, I wanted to live in a different culture outside the United States. I wanted to experience a little adventure. JVI was a great way to accomplish this.

I didn't choose to go to Palau, the JVI did. They decided the best fit was Palau, both for me and Palau. Which was good, because I never would have chosen Palau; I didn't even know Palau existed. When I first heard about Palau it was over the phone. I was told, "You're going to Palau." To me it sounded like, "You're going to plow."

"Hunh?" I responded.

A chuckle, then the explanation, "PAH… lauuu. It's an island nation in the western Pacific."

"Oh…"

The first thing I did was check an atlas. I never expected to live on a tropical island. But I was excited.

The day after the graduation ceremony for Mindszenty High School (named after a cardinal in Bulgaria), I was at the Fisheries Dock waiting for the *Suena* dingy. A few of my friends and a few of my students were with me, saying their last good-byes. I was a salad of emotions: sadness at leaving my home for the past six years, heartbreak at seeing my friends possibly for the last time, pride at having been called a "Palauan" by the islanders, and excitement to be embarking on an adventure.

One of my friends asked, "Which boat will you be on?"

I pointed to the white *Suena* in the harbor, about fifty yards off.

"You're going to sail across the ocean on that?" was the reply.

I nodded.

"But it's so tiny."

"It's thirty-six feet," I explained, trying to convince even myself that it was more than sufficient for an open ocean voyage.

"Aren't you scared?"

I shook my head confidently, but I could feel the butterflies in my stomach.

The dingy arrived, piloted by Phyllis. The last obligatory pictures were taken, good-byes were said, and hugs were exchanged. I loaded my three small bags and a bunch of bananas given by a friend as a parting gift on the dingy. I gingerly climbed in the dingy and rode to the *Suena* with Phyllis. Once on the *Suena* a last good-bye was yelled across the water accompanied by frantic arm-waving. Then the good-bye party drove off into the jungle, and I felt an important part of me go with them, leaving a void in my chest. Particularly painful was seeing one particular friend leave – Pilordes – for she, as is turned out, would one day be my wife.

The adrenaline and excitement of the impending adventure helped to keep the void at bay, and I was ready to get moving, largely to keep the adrenaline flowing. I wanted to keep busy to help dissipate my emptiness. But as with many things, everything isn't as simple as we would like them to be, or go as we would plan them. There was still much to learn before embarkation, and my lessons were to commence immediately. First, I had to broaden my knowledge of the boat itself.

The rear section of the sailboat – above deck – was called the cockpit. The *Suena* had no steering wheel like the ones most people associate with ships, but instead had a large tiller which could be operated in the cockpit. Beneath the cockpit floor lay the engine and storage, such as water and fuel and other miscellaneous items such as ropes, safety equipment, sails, fishing gear, et cetera… A small canopy at the fore of the cockpit provided shade from the intense tropical sun, and here was located the GPS and compass.

Below the canopy at the fore cockpit were three steps that descended into the cabin. The "steps" were more a ladder than steps. The cabin (below deck) of this thirty-six foot sailboat, as can be imagined, wasn't very spacious, which forced all available space to be used to maximum efficiency. The stairs were on hinges for engine access (under the cockpit). Just fore of the steps on the port side (left side, facing forward) was the map table and navigation aids. Opposite this, on the starboard side, was the galley (kitchen): four gimbaled propane burners, sink, foot pumps for water (both seawater and freshwater), minimum cupboard space aft, and storage under the sink. Just fore of the map table on the port side was the head; very tiny! About the size of a shower stall, but no shower, just a tiny toilet and a tinier sink. Opposite the head on the starboard side were storage cabinets mostly for personal items, such as clothes. Fore of all this was the "living area" of the cabin: a small room the width of the sailboat at its widest section. The main mast pole went through the center of the room; there were couches along the port, starboard and fore sides of the room; a small table attached to the mast pole that had fold-out sections for more table area; the radio equipment was on shelves above the port couch; personal storage and books on the other shelves above the couches; and storage (mostly food) under the couches and under floor panels. Fore of the main living area was a small, triangular sleeping space that occupied the front of the sailboat. This was Rick's and Phyllis's space. My bed was the starboard couch, which had straps to hold me in when the *Suena* pitched and rolled in the waves.

Although small, the cabin had a warm, homey feeling to it, and all necessities were present. I was amazed how a whole home could be crammed into such a small space, and still be surprisingly comfortable.

"We've cleared out some space for you," Rick informed me as we went down the three ladder stairs, bringing us below deck. "Be sure your things are secure if you don't want your stuff all over the cabin." Rick seemed like a good-natured guy, but he had a way – I found out quickly – to make simple "advice" sound like a threat. However, my excitement at that time was still abundant enough to filter out this seemingly negative aspect of Rick. And besides, I was still trying to impress on Rick and Phyllis that they had made the right choice in me as their crew member; I didn't even consider that his tone of voice might be the slightest bit improper.

I had enough time to throw my things on the couch – my bed – before Rick began with a flow of instructions, or, rather, rules and edicts. It was time for me to learn to be a crew member on a sailboat. Phyllis was also below deck at this time, and it was obvious that Rick's instructions were as much reminders for her as they were "lessons" for me. He didn't have any pattern to his lecture, he just discoursed on whatever caught his attention or popped into his head. There is a lot to a sailboat, and with his years of sailing experience, he had much to fill my eager – and novice – mind. Since we had planned to be on the open ocean by this time the next day, we didn't have the luxury of time. And being on a sailboat traveling over open ocean we had no luxury for mistakes. It was important I learn well and fast.

"You'll notice these handles about the cabin," he spoke, grabbing one for emphasis. "You'll want to be holding on to something at all times when we are at sea. Begin to familiarize yourself with all the handholds now, so you can find them in the dark – and you will need them in the dark." At the time his tone seemed unnecessarily harsh. But I could later appreciate the importance of his warnings that I couldn't then. I could also appreciate his use of a harsh tone – it may have irritated me, but that is precisely how it got my attention.

His discourses could have been divided into three parts: suggestions, instructions and rules. I've already given two examples of suggestions. Another one was, "It will be hot out at sea, so you will want to dress as lightly, and wear as little as possible. Personally, I prefer to go naked. I suggest you do the same, but I'll leave that up to you." I didn't follow this suggestion.

His instructions were mostly on skills I had to learn, like, "This is how you flush this toilet…" Or how to raise and lower sails, how to adjust sails, how to tie knots, what knots to tie and when, how to use the navigation system, how to keep on course, et cetera…

The rules included, "No wet clothes beyond this point [the bottom of the steps]." That meant, basically, no wet clothes below deck. This was another reason for going naked – no need to remove wet clothes, or dry them once removed. His rules were the easiest to distinguish from suggestions and instructions – rules had a sharper edge in his voice. "The propane valve – here – stays closed at all times, except when cooking. We don't want an explosion out at sea." I could definitely tell this was a rule from the chill that ran up my spine.

It wasn't long before my head was saturated, yet I continued nodding at everything he said. I was ready to begin doing something – the best mode for me to retain information and really understand.

My real desire was to get under way that very day, but there was much to do in preparing the *Suena* for our journey. Most of the important work that first day was done by Rick and Phyllis as they explained to me about the sailboat and its workings. However, I wasn't left idle; there was plenty for me to do also.

The large cockpit canopy used while anchored was taken down and stowed, and a smaller one for sailing was put in its place. Materials were stored away. The water tanks were filled with fresh water, and fuel tanks were topped off. Personal belongings were secured. Safety lines were tied in, and safety equipment was checked and put in accessible locations. The sails were unpacked and hanked to the stays, and sheets (ropes to control the sails) were tied on and run to the winches (which held the ropes tight). We worked for hours. This is what I needed and I welcomed the diversion.

Everything was checked twice. We were almost ready to go. Then Rick and I had to make one last trip to land. Rick thought we might stop at Helen's Reef, which was on the way from Palau to Australia. But he needed to secure official permission to stop there from the Helen's Reef and Tobi State Government. We also had to file exit papers.

Helen's Reef and Tobi were part of the Southwest Islands of Palau, which were located hundreds of miles to the southwest outside the archipelago of Palau proper. The furthest, Tobi, was almost three hundred miles distant. Also included were Merir and Sonsoral. Politically, these islands were included in the Republic, but culturally they were different. The Southwest islanders spoke a different language, which I was told was very similar to Chuukese, spoken in the islands of Chuuk, a few thousand miles to the east. Their culture was also more similar to Chuuk than Palau, and even the facial features of the Southwest Islanders were different than that of the Palauans.

Unfortunately, the Southwest Islanders were looked down upon by most Palauans. They were thought of as "outer islanders," sort of the "country folk" or the "simple" people of Palau, and thus they experienced prejudice. It confused me as to why these gentle and friendly people were discriminated against.

When I first arrived in Palau political tension was high. It was a time Palauans were voting on a referendum to pass, or not, something called the Compact of Free Association. This Compact was a political agreement with the United States that would give the U.S. some military rights on Palauan land and waters, and in return promised certain monetary compensations to Palau. Many Palauans believed that if the Compact were passed it would mean more money in their own pockets and a higher standard of living. But the clauses in the Compact regarding the military use of land (traditional and sacred) and the freedom for the U.S. to construct a port for nuclear naval vessels were reprehensible to many Palauans. The tension between these two views erupted into violence. The first few months I was in Palau there were bombings, arson of homes, and even fatal shootings as a result of these tensions. It was during this time that one of the legislators proposed legislation to remove the Southwest Islands from the Republic in an attempt to remove two of the fourteen Palauan States that were voting opposite what they desired. It was not only conniving, but malicious toward the Southwest Islanders. The violence frightened me, but the politics frightened me more.

Although I had visited one of the Southwest Islands – Sonsoral – for a short time (I was on the island less than six hours), I was excited that the *Suena* would be stopping there on our way to Australia. Even if only for a short time.

Rick and I arrived at the Helen's Reef/Tobi State office. We were only about a half of a mile from where the *Suena* was anchored. The office was only a few small rooms on the second floor of an old building that seemed mostly abandoned and smelled unused and musty. I could discern no organization in the office, and the only decorations were two posters showing native species of fish. In charge was a former

Peace Corps volunteer, Mike, who had married a local girl from Tobi island. He lived in Aiang, a village on Koror, when he wasn't on one of the Southwest Islands. He assured us everything was in order, and he gave Rick some supplies to deliver when we arrived on Helen's Reef. Mike wished us a good voyage, then we set off for the Palau Emigration Office, our last stop and "official" good-bye.

At Emigration no one answered our knocks to the door of the simple wooden building by the water, only about 100 yards from the *Suena*. The door was unlocked so we timidly entered the building. Inside it was bright from the many windows, bright white walls and sunny day. The squeaking roar of the air conditioner filled the room with a loud silence and a heavy coldness. Rick called out above the drone of the laboring machine, but with no desired response. Rick tentatively opened another door in the back of the room and disappeared beyond, looking for the emigration officers. I wandered over the worn, peeling, yellowed tiles, around the three, grey, government-issue desks, scattered with papers. The bright walls were tacked randomly with tide, airplane, and other odd schedules, along with torn and obviously much referred to maps. A map of Palau caught my eye. As I looked over the names of places on the map – Ngeraard, Melekeok, Airai, Ngeremeiaus, Ngemeliis – my mind was filled with images of each place, along with people I had met and known, and things I had done and experienced at each locale. It was a combination of thankfulness at having had those experiences and having known those people, and sadness at letting go. I looked at the map with affection, knowing that Palau was now more than a name on a map, but a place that now resided deep in my heart.

"Yes, I have all three passports," I heard Rick's voice say as the rear door opened, breaking my reverie. Rick followed the emigration officer through the door to one of the desks. The emigration officer was a man I had seen before on different occasions, but I didn't know him personally. When he caught sight of me his gaze lingered for a moment, and he seemed to be thinking the same thing. He wore a uniform with an official patch on the shoulder and breast, and a badge pinned to the front. The uniform would have made him look official except it was extremely faded and worn. It appeared the uniform shirt was the original issue, and he had worn no others – for years. Even the patches were faded and the shirt was too threadbare to hold a wrinkle.

As he sat down at the desk he casually began to arrange forms on the desk in front of him. He asked Rick questions about citizenship, length of stay, destinations, names, particulars about his sailboat, and more. As Rick answered, the emigration officer slowly and neatly wrote all the information in the proper places on the forms.

So much paperwork, I thought. I also thought what a shame it was that Palauans had adopted so many of our Western ways, which in my opinion, were of no benefit to their culture. Rick tried to make small-talk with the officer, but the officer would have nothing of it. A task needed to be done, and friendliness was not to get in the way. I returned to the map and continued to remember my years and experiences in Palau.

Thirty minutes after starting the emigration paperwork we were back on the *Suena*.

"Raise the anchor," Rick called out. It was an exciting moment. Phyllis showed me how to use the crank and I began pumping the crank handle, getting splattered with oil and seawater as the anchor chain rattled over the front pulley. We were finally going to begin the actual traveling – I was ready to go. I was a part of it. I wasn't just a passenger. I was part of the team, a crew member. And my straining at the anchor emphasized this fact. I said a prayer for safety and of thanksgiving as we began our journey.

We used the engine to motor out of the harbor and through a passage in the Rock Islands that would point us south – the direction that we would anchor for the night within protective reef and islands. Not much traveling for that first day – I would have rather been heading directly out to sea – but at least we were finally moving.

While we motored in the harbor my lessons continued. I was taught how to steer the boat and how to keep the boat on course. I was given the tiller and made a series of practice turns to specified compass headings. I feared doing it wrong, so I was timid, but with Rick and Phyllis's encouragement I was able to overcome my timidness, make a few mistakes, and learn what I needed to learn. I learned rapidly, and I was enjoying it to the full.

Once through that first passage we put up the sails – more lessons, more participation, more muscle straining, more excitement – and we were sailing! I had heard that sailing is an exceptionally freeing experience, and now I could say it was true. My first time ever sailing, and no getting off for 1500 miles!

When we were under way there really wasn't much to do except relax and enjoy; the sails, the automatic steering system operated by a wind-vane, and the wind did all the work. It was hard for me to relax because of me exhilaration, but the calm of the water, the glisten of the sun, the smell of the pure air, the motion of the sailboat, and the beauty of the Rock Islands made it hard not to become peaceful.

We were surrounded by the many Rock Islands – about 200 ranging in size from a small house to long skinny islands miles long, creating an intricate maze – and the water was calm, as it usually was inside the reef surrounding Palau. To the southeast I could see a number of Rock Islands that were beautiful to take a speedboat through. Not many beaches, but the views were spectacular. And although the beaches were scarce, this didn't mean there were no places to go.

I remembered the many times I had been through there. Near a natural arch – a common sight pointed out to tourists – was a location that had some soft corral. One afternoon a year or two earlier, coming back from a picnic with students, the boat driver stopped at the soft corral spot. I borrowed a mask and with the others I dove in and checked it out. Everywhere in Palau the underwater scenes were astounding, and the soft corral was no different. Not that deep, so I could free dive to see the sights.

We weren't in a hurry and there was time for some swimming, which we all did. The water in Palau was perfect for swimming all the time, and was never cold.

I had been swimming for awhile when I looked up and saw a number of teenagers climbing up a cliff face. With the nature of the limestone uplifts there were a number of handholds and footholds, but a rope had been anchored to the cliff face for assistance; obviously someone had been here before and this was a climb that must have had some interest. Even though I had been to this cove before I had never seen that rope. The rope brought the students about twenty feet above the water, and then they were skirting the edge of the cliff along a narrow ledge. They were congregating at a point that was ideal for jumping into the water. It was obvious that once at the jumping off point many students were having second thoughts about jumping, yet none were heading back to the rope; I'm sure that would have been too much of a disgrace for a teenager. When they gathered enough courage a teenager would step up to a small natural platform in the rock, take a few deep breaths, then jump, or, rather, step into the void. They seemed to be in the air quite a while, then splash! A few seconds later they would surface, their face lit up with excitement and exhilaration. It was a joy watching the students have so much fun.

I'm not sure how it happened, but I soon found myself climbing the cliff with the help of the rope. The "trail" up the cliff was established, but the limestone was still very sharp. I did not have any footwear, which made it very difficult on the sharp rock, but I was determined to make it, cuts and scratches or not. Once on top I immediately knew why students were hesitating to leap from the cliff; it was a long way down, much longer than it seemed from below. It was scary up there! I considered retreating and going back down the rope, but it would have been too much of a shame for me also.

There were about eight or ten students up there with me, all of us clinging to the sharp cliff face. More were making their way up the ropes. I knew I had to jump, and my heart was racing as I struggled to gather up the courage. As it got more crowded the students began playing a game that went like this: When one student jumped, he or she would – mid-air – call the name of another student, who had to jump next. It wasn't long before my name was called.

So without protesting or hesitation – in the spirit of the game – I stepped up to the ledge. I looked down at the water. I knew it was about a twenty foot drop, but it seemed like much further. I knew I couldn't think about it too long or I would lose my courage, so without thinking I stepped into the void.

What a feeling! I'm sure my heart stopped, and it seemed like I was in the air for the longest time. Later I used a calculator just to see how long I was in the air: about a second and a half. I was a little surprised because I think I said the entire Our Father while falling! When I finally hit the water and came up alive it as such an exhilarating feeling – I felt so alive! Part of the feeling was that I had survived and had no injuries, but the other part was that I had conquered the cliff. And since I had done it I didn't have to do it again.

So imagine my surprise when I found myself climbing the rope again. The second time up top, surprisingly, was as scary as the first. I asked my self, *What the heck am I doing up here a second time!?!* The second jump was a little easier, but just as exhilarating.

I was beginning to question my sanity when I was up top a third time, but at least this time I knew I could do it so I was considerably less nervous. This was going to be the last time, of course. I was going to jump this last time and call it a day. Willie, my friend and the other adult on the trip, was also up there with me. Then he said the words I didn't want to hear, "I'm going to dive this time." Not that we were having a competition, but I knew this meant I would have to dive also. He dove. It wasn't a perfect dive, but it was a dive. From a cliff twenty feet up. I had to push my own limits. For my own peace of mind. The original fear was back, and stronger. I stepped up to the leaping point. I looked down. The longest ever. I thought how I had to enter the water and how important it was to keep my arms together. This was all about conquering my fear and asserting my confidence. I thought one last time about how I had to enter the water, then without hesitating – which would have been death – I leapt from the cliff. It was a long second and a half. Then I plunged into the water, and I went deep. The exhilaration was instant and strong. I emerged to the surface with a gasp of breath and a sense of victory. Certainly not a perfect dive, but I had done it. And the cheers were welcome.

The fourth time on top wasn't really a surprise. I wanted to do a better dive. And I did. I probably would have gone back for more, but the boat was preparing to leave. Probably just as well before I injured myself from exhaustion.

As the *Suena* sailed toward Oolong, where we would spend our last night in Palau, I remembered all the times I had traveled this route by speedboat, and how different it was by sailboat: I couldn't help but to reminisce about my times at the Rock Islands as they moved past us: the picnics, the parties, the adventures, the people. These islands were beautiful, as Rick and Phyllis attested to, but for me they were not only physically beautiful, they were a part of my soul and I was a part of them. I could feel their hold on my heart as we quietly sailed past on the *Suena*. And it wouldn't be easy to resist that hold.

So there I was the next morning, standing on the deck of the *Suena*, ready to sail out of Palau and on to Australia, finding it hard to believe both that I was leaving Palau after so many years and that I was actually doing something I had only before dreamed about.

I enjoyed some quiet time alone with the water, birds breeze and Rock Islands in the morning light. It was still early when Rick and Phyllis got up. We had a cooked breakfast together; they told me that we should take advantage of the calm, for a day later we would be on the open ocean and, although cooking breakfast would still be possible, the effort wouldn't be worth the trouble in a constantly moving boat. Also, we would be on our watch schedules and the times would be rare when all three of us would be together. It was a nice breakfast, but I felt a pressure to get going.

It was a fairly quick breakfast, for we did have at least one time constraint – the tide. We had to get out of that Rock Island cove before the water was so low it wouldn't allow the keel to pass over the shallow passage. I didn't want to miss that.

We finished our meal together and checked everything one last time. We were soon out of the cove and moving. It was a beautiful day, not a cloud in the sky. But there was also no wind. That was okay according to Rick – he didn't expect to be under sail until we were outside the reef of the archipelago anyway. So we motored through the Rock Islands toward the south.

But there was another problem. Rick began to set the GPS but it wasn't working right. There seemed to be moisture in the LCD screen. He thought it might be okay when it dried out. But there was no way to be sure, until we were out to sea. And what if the moisture was also in the circuits? Rick could navigate without it, but it would be much more risky and difficult, especially approaching the narrow straights just east of New Guinea and later into Darwin. What to do? Take a risk, hope for the best? Of course I was anxious to get out into the open ocean, but I wasn't captain, so thankfully, I didn't have to make that decision. Rick and Phyllis discussed it for a few moments. I listened but didn't offer any opinion. It wasn't my place. Yet.

"Go back to Koror," Rick finally decided. He knew of another sailboat he could borrow a navigation system from. So off – in the wrong direction from our final goal – we motored, slowly. This was already taking longer than I had hoped. My spirits were dampened.

By speed boat the trip would have taken 30 to 45 minutes, but at our present rate on the *Suena*, it would be closer to two hours. So I had nothing to do but to relax and think. For me, I associate Koror with the Catholic Mission, where I had been a part for the past six years. I was remembering a letter I had sent home expressing the flavor of life on Palau, particularly in the Catholic Mission. The letter went (in part) like this …

I and the other guys were eating dinner at the Priests' house[1] *the other evening, when, as usual, Dave and Brother Walter got into it. I particularly blame Dave, for he intentionally tries to irritate Brother Walter, and more likely than not he succeeds. Brother Walter isn't exceptionally adept at logical argument, and Dave uses this to his advantage, regularly arguing circles around Brother Walter, who just gets more and more flustered. All to Dave's glee, of course. Usually their spats revolve around politics, Brother Walter being a stanch republican and Dave a democrat, but on this particular evening the argument of the day regarded stoves.*

The cook was off that night so the meal was light. Afterwards Dave decided that he was still hungry, but wasn't sure if he wanted to go to the trouble to prepare some ramen for himself. Partly, Dave was just impatient and didn't want to wait for the water to boil. On hearing this, a big grin grew on Brother Walter's face, and he said, "Well, Dave, you don't have to worry about nothin', because we got here the fastest stove in the west. This stove'll get yer water boilin' licity-split!" Brother Walter was genuinely pleased, which was evidenced by the increase of spraying spittle when he spoke.

[1] Being a teacher at the Catholic Mission school I and two other teachers shared an apartment above the school. Three times a week we were invited to eat with the Priests, who resided across the street in a house near the church.

*Dave thinks he can get Brother Walter's goat, but on occasion it is the other way around, and I suspect this was one of those times. Dave's face also sprouted a big smile, and I could see mischievousness written all over it. "But Brother," Dave said with just a dash of evil, "**We** have the fastest stove in the West."*

"No," Brother stated matter-of-factly, holding his ground. "This stove will boil water faster than any stove in Koror."

*I could hear the jest in Dave's voice when he said, "No, Brother Walter, I know **our** stove can boil water faster than this one."*

*Unfortunately, Brother Walter couldn't hear the same jest in Dave's voice, and he replied to Dave with some gravity, "I'd bet on it. This stove will boil water faster than **any** stove in Koror, hands down. Including yours!"*

*"You'd **bet** on it, Brother Walter?" Dave asked in a way that sounded like a threat.*

"Yes!"

*"Then maybe we need to have a little wager, see who's stove really **is** fastest."*

*"You're on." There was fire in Brother's Walter's eyes by this time, and Dave wasn't doing anything to put that fire out. In fact the fire had spread to Dave, too. The rest of us were shaking our heads and saying to ourselves, "Not **again** . . . "*

I suppose the easiest way to have resolved this was to have Brother Walter visit our kitchen with a stopwatch, time how long it would take our stove to boil water and compare it to his own. But no, that was not to be. Dave got Brother Walter riled up, which in turn got himself riled up too, and it had to be a "contest."

I suppose living somewhere other than on a remote pacific island people wouldn't have had time for such a contest, but Brother Walter and Dave both managed to enlist the services of quite a few people to pull off the Stove Boiling Contest, as it came to be known.

The contest occurred one week later on a Sunday afternoon, as Sundays tended to be uneventful and most people were free for "frivolousness."

They had gotten a friend of the priest's who was a senator in the Palauan government to be the official judge, plus four others to volunteer to ensure all was on the up-n-up. The two houses were less than 150 yards apart, so the Senator stood in the field halfway between the two houses. Each stove location had two judge's assistants, one to verify start times and boiling times, and the other to communicate all information and progress to the Senator.

Of course, before starting a few ground rules had to be set and criteria determined. For instance, it was decided that the amount of water was to be exactly one quart. Being the science teacher, I had to measure the water precisely for each location, watched by the judge's assistants for verification. The water had to be taken from the same source so it would be the same temperature and would have similar "impurities," if they existed. Also, we had to find two pans that were as close to identical as possible. This took a little doing, asking a lot of people, but because there were only a few stores on the island that sold such items, it was in the end pretty easy to find two pans that were the same.

The big question was, how do you define "boiling"? Again, being the science teacher they turned to me to come up with a definition. This was not easy, because if you have ever watched water boil you know that first you see steam, which is almost imperceptible at first but then increases dramatically. Also, you see tiny bubbles form, which increase in number and size, then some slowly float up, which, again, increase to a dramatic roiling, turbulent boiling. At which point do you ***definitively*** *say boiling has started? Since this was a boiling race, "boiling" had to be defined quite accurately. In the end it was agreed that boiling would be defined when the perturbations of the boiling water were exactly half an inch above the surface of the water at rest. We actually – or, rather, I – made "indicators" which were placed on the pan that had a piece of cardboard that rested exactly one half inch above the surface of the resting water. This took some doing, and I spent a few hours preparing these "boiling indicators."*

Did it have to be this complicated? Apparently yes, because both Dave and Brother Walter were driving it to the nth degree.

*On the day of the Stove Boiling Contest all preparations were meticulously made, judge's watching and verifying each and every step. Finally all was in place. The Senator, standing in the field between the two houses with a stopwatch and about twenty spectators (plus the 15 or so elders who are regulars on Sunday afternoons sat outside the Church chewing betelnut), raised his hand and yelled, "On your mark, get set, **GO**!" dropping his hand. At seeing the hand drop, the judge's communicator assistants yelled "Go!" to each stove participant, who then turned on his respective stove.*

I have to admit that it was pretty exciting… until then, at which point we just had to wait.

The stoves heated up, then the water started to emit tiny wisps of vapor and tiny bubbles formed on the bottoms and sides of the pans. The judge's assistants yelled progress to the Senator in the field. Then it started to get exciting again… the water was beginning to steam pretty heavily and the bubbles grew larger and began to float up to the surface, causing the surface to undulate. Boiling would soon follow!

But it never seemed to progress beyond this point. There were still bubbles and steam, but the boiling didn't come. We wondered what was the problem and Dave began to worry that Brother Walter was going to win. We listened to the reports from the other side, but it seemed like they too were not having any further progress either.

Then we knew, and just to be sure someone turned on the light switch. Nothing. The electricity had gone out. Not unusual in Palau.

We hoped it would come back on, and we waited. But we couldn't make the Senator wait all afternoon in the church field. After about an hour we had to call it quits.

That night at dinner at the priest's house there was a lot of animated talk, mostly from Brother Walter. He insisted his pot was on the verge of a full boil. He was very excited, again indicated by the amount of spittle spewing forward. Dave, of course, claimed the same, and the matter went unresolved. They promised they would try again soon, but to date nothing has materialized, and Brother Walter and Dave continue to boil over with boasts about their stoves.

On a few occasions I sent "newsletter" type of letters to a number of friends and family back home, and this was one of them. I am constantly amazed at what people will do in the name of competition. I was also surprised that this letter got the most replies, and most people were dying to know who finally won the Stove Boiling Contest.

Chapter 2

The Dream of Sailing

It was early afternoon when we were sailing out of the Koror channel – a different exit from Palau than we had originally planned, but neither had we planned on GPS problems. We had picked up a spare GPS from another sailboat in case Rick's GPS failed (his was working, again). We were heading east-southeast out through the Koror Channel – a quicker way to exit the surrounding reef. There was a stiff wind and our sails were full. The channel – dredged through coral for boat passage to the main Koror dock – was narrow with shallow reef on either side, so tacking through the channel was a delicate operation. This was my first real experience at working as a team, as a crew member on the *Suena*.

I could see Rick's body tense as we began our maneuvers, and his voice took on a different quality, belying the strain he was experiencing as captain. I didn't then fully appreciate his nervousness, nor the importance that his whole home and well-being were being threatened by the beautiful, yet dangerous, reef only feet from everything he owned.

Rick stood at the prow of his vessel while Phyllis and I worked the sheets upon his commands. Phyllis was holding the tiller on the course Rick indicated, while I prepared the sheets for a tack. I, myself, was tense for two reasons: I could feel the tenseness in the air from Rick, and I wanted to do my own job correctly – this was my first real sailing test and I wanted to pass.

"Prepare to tack!" Rick yelled from the bow. His voice sounded angry.

I unhitched the port sheet from the cleat, which held the sheet tightly in place. And, although the sheet was still wrapped around the winch three times (it would have been impossible to hold otherwise), I could feel the rope straining to pull free as I held it tightly in my hand, but my adrenalin gave me the needed strength to keep it tight. Phyllis calmly explained – again – what I should do when the time came. Her words and tone were more reassuring than instructional.

"When I say 'Now!' tack!" Rick shouted with more volume than necessary.

The *Suena* quietly cut through the water while Phyllis and I waited tensely the few seemingly long moments for Rick's command.

"Now!" Rick finally screamed.

Phyllis swung the tiller hard to the port side and the *Suena* responded. "Release the sheet," Phyllis said. I ducked as the boom swung over my head.

"Tack! Release the sheet!" Rick screamed hoarsely.

With nervousness and uncertainty I began to let out the sheet, trying to control its speed so there wouldn't be an override (when the rope essential wraps over itself and tangles, which would be really bad), which Rick warned me so harshly about earlier.

"Faster!" Rick commanded.

Phyllis leapt to the other crank and began pulling in the starboard sheet as fast as she could. When it became tight she started cranking the winch by hand to continue bringing in the sheet.

I was trying to judge if the port sheet was safe from override when I heard Rick shout at me, "Help Phyllis!" I made sure the port sheet was free then jumped to help Phyllis. I pulled on the rope as Phyllis cranked the sheet tight.

"More!" Rick yelled.

Phyllis and I switched; I cranked and she held the rope. I could feel my muscles straining as I cranked. It seemed tight, but Rick kept yelling, "More! More!"

Finally the tack was complete, the *Suena* cutting smoothly through the water in a new direction. Phyllis was standing, tiller in hand, while I finished securing the sheet on the cleat. My heart was racing and I could feel adrenalin pumping into my system – much stronger than a morning cup of black coffee!

Rick yell a reprimand at us for our slow work. Phyllis said quietly to me, "You did fine, but don't be afraid to let out the sheet faster."

Despite Phyllis' reassurances, I felt disgraced from Rick's scolding. I should have done better. I was determined to do better next time, and that next time was approaching rapidly.

I prepared the port sheet for reeling in, my heart still racing, the adrenalin not letting up. I repeatedly reviewed in my head what I would do and how I would do it better this time, how I could do it faster, cleaner.

Phyllis spoke in calm voice, "It's okay to let the rope out faster," then Rick yelled, "Prepare to tack!"

I positioned myself on the starboard crank, unhitched the sheet, preparing for the release. My body was tense.

"Now!"

Phyllis swung the tiller hard to the starboard side and grabbed the port sheet. The boom swung over my head. I began releasing the sheet as fast as I deemed safe. Rick was yelling for speed. Phyllis was frantically pulling in the other sheet, coils of rope piling up on her side of the cockpit and flying out from my side.

"Faster!"

When safe I let go of my sheet and jumped to assist Phyllis. I grabbed the crank and cranked like crazy, Phyllis pulling the loose rope and guiding the tiller.

Again, my muscles were straining. They were getting tired. Isn't that enough, I wondered as I felt my muscles about to collapse.

"More!"

I found more energy to crank two more times, and I wondered if I could manage a third, but Rick said, "Okay."

He again reprimanded us for our sloth.

Can I keep this up? I wondered. It was much more straining that I had anticipated. I glimpsed ahead as I secured the sheet and moved to prepare the other; we were maybe a third of the way through the channel. I have to do it! I reprimanded myself for doubting.

I had a few minutes of rest before the next tack. I was nervous, afraid of failing, afraid of more of Rick's acid scolding, afraid of not having what it takes – on this first test! Yet I also found myself filled with exhilaration. I'm sailing! I thought.

The rest of the channel passage was about the same. By the last tack I had improved – I could feel it, and Phyllis assured me this was in fact true – but Rick continued to have harsh words to say during and after each tack. It seemed to have gone smooth, though, no mishaps, no close calls, no contacts with reef.

When I had time to review things later I could understand Rick's tenseness, and I could understand his strong words – it was his boat, his house, his livelihood. And I had to admit that I probably learned better and faster with strong words on my performance, the intensity made me perform. What I wondered, though, was his degree of harshness necessary? He seemed so angry, so offended, so intense as if we were on the very edge of total destruction. The moment should have been tense, no doubt, but was it too much? It seemed that way to me, but I was too much of a novice to really know for sure.

I was stung by Rick's harsh tone, but Phyllis assured me I had done well. Somehow the two viewpoints helped me to come to a balance of pressure to perform well, and reassurance that I wasn't a complete failure.

We were soon free of the channel and in deeper water. We were on course to leave the final ring of reef, which meant, for all practical purposes, we were on our way! The day was still beautiful, but now we had, in addition to the beautiful sun and sky, a steady wind, calm waters, and a working GPS (with a backup!). We had discussed watches earlier – I was left with the noon till 4 pm and midnight till 4 am watches – so Rick, after being convinced everything was sailing smoothly, went below deck to get some sleep. I was on watch!

I found that sailing is exceptionally relaxing, and at times mundane with its uneventfulness. The movie "Wind" of course is about racing which is very different than travel sailing, and the move crams into one hour the excitement of months. In real sailing, once things are set and going there's not much to keep one busy, as I was experiencing on my first watch. But there is also something ethereal, peaceful, spiritual and mystical about sailing that makes up for the mundane-ness of it. I was not at all disappointed with sailing there on my first watch. In fact, I never tired of the sailing at any point in the voyage.

Without the excitement and pressure of the tacking through the narrow channel leaving Koror, I was now able to feel the weight of responsibility I had while on watch – it was now my job to identify any dangers and act on them. I had to keep the sailboat on course. I had to monitor the weather, look for floating debris that could damage the boat. I also felt the magnitude of the crossing we were about to make. We would be crossing open ocean and far any from help, if needed promptly. This filled me with a measure of excitement, and a bit of anxiousness. I was also discovering how beautiful it was to be out on the open water. Palau was still in view, as it would be for most of the day, and that gave me a special feeling of being still at home, and the beauty of it was still touching me deeply as I viewed it from a different perspective. Also, the motion of the boat as it cut through the water, the vastness and mystery of the water, the caress of the wind, the sparkle of the sun, the blue of the sky, the closeness of Palau, the quiet, the knowledge of the boundless life unseen below us, the uncertainty of what adventures we would encounter ahead all added to my excitement and enjoyment of the peaceful watch. I was filled with awe at all that I was taking in, at this different perspective that I was allowed to experience life from. I was on one of the pinnacles of life, and I felt blessed.

But with the excitement gone of getting ready and the excitement gone of tacking through the Koror Channel I started to think about Palau, and I started to miss it immediately. My thoughts began to drift to Pilordes, my "friend" back in Koror.

I met her in the Sacred Heart Catholic Church choir, which I had led for the six years I had been in Koror. One day there were two new members, and one was Pilordes. It wasn't often that we got new members in the choir. I welcomed them and tried to help them feel comfortable. I couldn't help but think, however, how pretty

Pilordes was. Such a nice smile, and I learned that first practice that she had a great sense of humor. I liked her and we seemed to "click" right away. I must admit that the thought did cross my mind, *I wonder if I could get her to marry me?* It was really kind of a joke to myself, partly because I was not a ladies man, but mostly because Pilordes was a nun.

But I decided not to dwell on these thoughts. Being my first watch and my first time sailing in open water, I was also filled with nervous energy. I checked all the things I was told to check – our course, the sails, the GPS, the solar panel – about three times more often than needed. The repetition was good, however, because it helped me become more familiar with the *Suena* and my responsibilities. I kept an almost constant scan of the horizon for other boats. There were none, except the rusting ship grounded on some reef off the starboard side, reminding captains of the dangerous reef just below the water. With all the time I had I examined everything in sight (especially the shipwreck) with binoculars. I walked around the sailboat, getting my sea legs, making myself as familiar as possible with everything on this new world I was living in, fascinated by the sails, the ropes and lines, and especially the flow of water as the wind pushed the sailboat ever onward. There is something enthralling about water in motion – a stream, waves crashing on a beach, a sailboat moving through water. I was finding the motion of the water was already casting its spell on me during that first watch, and it was a comfort to me throughout the trip.

My watch went without a hitch. Phyllis was above deck during most of my watch, watching me (in a very non-threatening manner), continuing with my lessons. I (with help) had to change course once, and adjustments on our heading were made only a few times. The rest of the time Phyllis read while I soaked in as much of my surroundings as I could, and getting as much of my last glimpse of Palau as possible. I used the binoculars to search the Rock Islands as we slowly moved past. Because we were on the outside of the reef I could not see the interior islands. But I was using familiar reference points to "see" the islands on the other side, remembering times I spent at the Rock Islands.

At one point I knew on the other side of the islands I was looking at was the island of Babelyoulmekang, where I had gone for a number of picnics with students and friends. On one particular occasion after spending the night and a morning of swimming and playing, then a lunch of local foods, my friend Willie said, "Let's go for a hike." I was tired, but sleep and rest would have to wait.

Willie started off in the opposite direction of the beach and into the jungle. We walked along a trail I hadn't noticed before. It wasn't much of a trail because much of it was overgrown with vines and ferns. I had to be especially careful since I was wearing zorries – thin, slippery rubber "flip-flops" – and a slip onto the sharp, ubiquitous limestone would be very painful. It wasn't long before light was vastly diminished as we got deeper into the thick vegetation. If it wasn't sharp limestone, we were stepping over and maneuvering over gnarled roots and through hanging vines. We started up a hill that soon became quite steep, which required "hiking" with hands as well as feet.

After about fifteen minutes we reached a crest, which we then began to descend. From our vantage point we could see that we were moving toward a large "lake" – it was actually a large inlet from the sea – ringed completely by steep Rock Islands. The descent was steeper than the ascent, but not terribly difficult because the limestone and roots allowed many foot and hand holds. As we neared the water we could see that limestone was close to vertical as it entered the water, and because of the clarity of the water we could see it was quite deep. So the easiest way to cover the last few feet was to just jump, which we did. The water felt great after the hike, cool and wet. And salty. Definitely sea water, not a freshwater lake, although from where we were we could not see the sea.

I knew I was in a very special place. How many times in my life would I be able to swim in paradise? The beauty was indescribable. The peacefulness was palpable. My joy was deep.

We leisurely swam about 100 yards through the lake to the inlet on the western edge. The inlet was really a tunnel, arched over by limestone and vegetation, that gave access to the sea. We were able to swim safely through the tunnel. On the other side we saw the familiar sight of the ocean. A number of speed boats passed in the distance, most probably taking Japanese tourists diving. The sound of the speedboats brought me back to reality, and I began to miss the quietness of the "lake" already. I was sure those tourists hadn't seen anything close to the beauty I had seen, nor appreciated it half as much.

We walked on limestone along the edge of the island, which was possible since the tide was low, and we made our way back to our boat. On the way we passed a small cave. Someone suggested we go inside, so we did. It wasn't a deep cave, but had a very high ceiling. "Look at that!" someone said, pointing at the ceiling. At first I didn't see anything, but then I could see it. Bats hanging on the rock above. All upside-down. Hundreds of them.

They must have heard us because they started to fly, one by one dropping off the ceiling, taking to flight. They were chirping, individually not tremendously loud, but then there were hundreds making noise. As they took to flight they circled around the top of the cave, and soon there was a whirlpool of bats going 'round and 'round in the space above us.

"Give me your shirt," Willie said to me. I was the only person wearing a shirt (that could be taken off) since I needed that extra protection against the sun. I gave Willie my shirt. He looked up at the whirlpool of bats, then adjusted the shirt in his hands. He threw the shirt up like a Frisbee, vertically, into the midst of the swarm of the chirping bats. When the shirt came back, inside was a small bat, not much bigger than a hummingbird. It looked scared, but Willie held it gently. "Wow!" was all I could say. Willie released the bat back into the whirlpool.

Standing on the *Suena*, still essentially in Palau with all my memories, I had some nervous energy that I wanted to expend. Normally I would have gone for a run, but that wasn't an option on the sailboat. So I continued to move around the boat, familiarizing myself with the *Suena* and its movement in the water. I also talked with Phyllis during her reading breaks, getting to know her better.

Later in the afternoon we passed Anguar, and I watched it a long time as it receded into the distance. This was the southernmost island of the main Palau archipelago. Anguar was not in the reef that surrounded the other islands, but about 10 miles south of the protective reef. You could get to Anguar from Koror by speedboat, but it took a long time – about two hours – and the boat driver had to be good, because you had to leave the protective reef of the main group and cross through the large swells and currents of the open ocean between the protective reef and the island. The Anguar dock was on the south end of the island, which meant circling around the island, making the trip even longer. Anguar also had an airport. I had the pleasure of traveling to Anguar by small plane, speedboat and slow-boat. Speedboat was the most exciting because of the ocean swells, unlike the often glass-like waters inside the reef. On top of a swell you could see quite far, but when the speedboat was between swells – in the trough – the only thing visible was walls of water on either side of the boat, and all sightings of land disappeared. It was an eerie feeling at first, but I also found I loved it.

I had the pleasure of bringing my sister to Palau when she visited. We stayed with the family of one of my students in a guest house that was very simple and clean, and our hosts were very generous. One afternoon we borrowed two bicycles to take a tour of the island. We took our time and circled the entire island in under three hours. On the west end we stopped in an area that was similar to rainforest: large trees with a high canopy, very humid with dew drops falling from the foliage above. We could hear the famous "Anguar Monkey" screeching high up in the trees. They knew we were there and we could hear their warning screams, and they stayed high in the canopy to avoid being seen. The monkeys were not actually indigenous to

Angaur, but had been brought to the islands as pets during the time of the Germans. Of course some had escaped and gone feral, becoming the Angaur monkey.

After getting a few micro-glimpses of the monkeys we continued on. We later found a turn off from the main road – really a disintegrating and old paved road that vegetation had mostly overtaken – and we followed a barely discernable trail and presently were at a World War II plane grave yard. It was like a neglected museum of old planes and plane parts. Having earned my degree in aerospace engineering, this was very fascinating for me. I loved looking at the old engines, bent propellers, wings, control surfaces, cockpits and more. The structure that was visible in the different parts was captivating. I could sit in a cockpit and imagine the fierce WWII battles that took place in Palau, especially famous for the battle of Peliliu (one of the Palauan islands which could be seen in the distance to the North). I felt bad for my sister who had little interest in such lore, so after about twenty minutes we reluctantly moved on.

The afternoon had progressed and the crabs began to come out. Once a month the crabs would come out as part of a mating instinct that was linked to the phases of the moon. We just happened to be there during the right time of the cycle. It was interesting at first, but became annoying when there were so many crabs crossing the road that it was hard to avoid hitting them on our bicycles. They slowed our progress considerably as we weaved in and out of the migrating crabs. If we came too close to a crab, it would raise its claws in a threatening gesture. Of course we wanted to do them no harm, but occasionally we would hear the crunch of the claw of a crab as our dodging wasn't successful, sending a shiver up our spines. It was a relief when we got back to the village.

We had arrived just in time to join the *machases* (older and respected Palauan women) as they were about to embark on some crab hunting.

"Would you and your sister like to go with us?" they asked.

"Sure."

We climbed into the back of a dilapidated pickup with four sixty-ish women and off we went, the women chattering and laughing the whole time. It wasn't long before the truck stopped. The women jumped out of the back of the truck with burlap sacks, still chattering and laughing. They began to deftly grab crabs and deposit them into the burlap sacks. Some of the women, very experienced, would just step behind a crab and grab it with forefinger and thumb, lift it and throw it in the sack. Others would first step on the back of the crab, immobilizing it, then grab it the same way, then drop it in the sack.

We stopped about four or five times before the sacks were full of crabs. As we drove back to the village, the sacks undulated eerily with a weird scraping sound as the crabs tried to escape. Once back in the village, large pots of water were already boiling on open fires. My sister and I feeling sweaty from the day's journey, excused ourselves to shower and freshen up. When we were finished the crab feast was ready. We were given a large plate of freshly boiled crab claws, and a bowl of melted butter. A few stones to crack the shells, and we were eating the freshest crab I have ever eaten. It was a seafood feast that beat any seafood meal I had had up to that point… or since. It was nice to share this with my sister. I only wish I could have also shared it with Dad.

From the *Suena*, remembering, I watched Angaur until the last remnants of it disappeared in the waves.

I got Rick up for his watch at 4:00 pm. I was now free; my watch was over. I wasn't ready for sleep, however, so I stayed above deck with Rick and Phyllis for conversation. It was a very pleasant time.

Rick, I learned, had traveled extensively, mostly through Southeast Asia and the islands of Asia, Malaysia, Indonesia and the Pacific. He had spent a year out of college traveling, living, studying and writing about his experiences. He also had a Master's degree in economics and had taught college in New Zealand and Australia. He had bought his sailboat almost eight years before. He lived on his boat while teaching, saving money for his next adventure.

Phyllis had a Master's degree in nursing. She traveled quite a bit also, mostly doing nursing related work, like training. Her hobby was telling stories. After ten minutes of talking with her I would describe her as a feminist, comfortable, not overbearing. She and Rick had met in New Zealand and had been traveling on the *Suena* for about a year prior to this journey. This, I was told, was their last journey together; once in Australia she was to go back to the States while he would look for work in Australia.

We talked until dinner time. We had agreed to rotate cooking duties, and whomever didn't cook would share cleanup and washing the dishes. Rick volunteered to cook that first evening. Looking back I could see that his volunteering that first night wasn't a purely altruistic offering; the seas were calm thus making cooking easy. I would recognize this ploy only after experience.

The dinner was good because it included fresh vegetables and cold drinks – we had to take advantage of fresh things while they were still fresh, and cold things while ice lasted in the ice-box. After dinner Phyllis and I did teamwork on the dishes. We finished just before sunset. It was so beautiful out! The sky was clear that exhibited a spectrum of mystical blue across the dome above, there were enough clouds near the horizon to be painted by the last brilliant colors of the sinking sun, reflecting off a very calm, undulating sea. It was such a peaceful time of day, and to be on a sailboat in the middle of a calm ocean! The night was cool and we had enough wind which kept the *Suena* sailing at a decent clip. By this time there was no land in sight.

Phyllis made us each a Bloody Mary, which we sipped on the deck, watching the sun dip into the water, giving a spectacular show. Rick said, "There may be too many clouds tonight, but we still might see the green flash."

"What's the green flash?" I asked.

"If you watch the horizon the instant the sun goes below it," he explained, "and the conditions are just right, you see a green flash."

"A green flash?" I repeated.

"Yes. It is soooo cool."

"I've never been able to see it," Phyllis admitted.

"You just don't know how to do it," Rick teased, but it was evident Phyllis didn't like his teasing.

I tried not to blind myself as I watched the sun dip below the horizon. I didn't see anything, but as soon as the sun went down Rick yelled, "YES!" and jumped up and down yelling, "Did you see it! That was GREAT!"

Phyllis looked at me and shrugged her shoulders.

I looked for it many times, but only on two occasions – once on the *Suena* and the other time in Saipan – I saw a bright green line along the horizon the instant the sun disappeared. I think this was the "green flash." For me it was not a flash, just a green line. It was still cool, though.

The *Suena* cut quietly and smoothly through the water while the wind, the sails and the boat did all the work and we relaxed, watching the stars begin to wink in to the darkening sky. It was such a tranquil time, and drinks with the sunset after dinner became a comfortable ritual throughout the voyage. I could hardly believe I had the wonderful luck (or karma) to be there at that moment. Sailing was wonderful!

I stayed above deck about another hour after the sun had set – I was still entranced with the beauty around me! With no lights around and clear sky the stars and night sky were beautiful. And the night water was glorious.

I knew I should get some sleep since I had watch again at midnight, but I was too wound up and ecstatic to sleep. I did go below and I lay on the couch that was my bed, and since I could not sleep I tried to read. But I wanted to tell Pilordes what sailing was like, share with her my excitement. But I couldn't, so I wrote some in my journal.

In Koror I had often gone to daily Mass at the church. It was convenient since the church was across the street, and I could hear the bells so I always knew when to go. Daily Mass was a nice thing because it helped me to wind down and be quiet after my busy days, and it gave me some time to think about what happened in my day, what I did good, what I could have done better, and so on. It also, however, gave me a time to see Pilordes. She went to Mass every day as part of her religious commitment as a nun. I think I always noticed her first in the church, and seeing her gave me a sense of calm in my heart. Sometimes when the sisters had Mass at their residence I would feel an emptiness in the church, and I looked forward to the next day when I could see her in Mass again.

I didn't attend Mass everyday, though. Sometimes I just needed a break or I had something to do. And sometimes I attended Mass in the Novitiate where there was usually Mass at the same time for the few novices (young men training to be come priests) who stayed at the Catholic Mission. I had become friends with these guys and ate dinner with them when we volunteers ate at the priests' house. I must admit, however, my Mass attendance at the church increased after I met Pilordes.

After Mass was a nice time to sit outside the church and enjoy the remnants of the sunset -- sunsets had become a hobby for me in Palau – and talk with whomever was present. Fortunately for me this usually meant time to talk with Pilordes. Conversation with her was always easy and comfortable, and I began to feel I could share anything with her. I often shared my struggles from my day, and my successes, and my hopes and dreams, and whatever came to mind. It gave me energy. I really began to love Mass! I was wishing at this time while on the *Suena* I could talk with her.

I laid down to sleep, but I only managed to doze a little before Phyllis informed me it was time for my watch in five minutes. I had done my first watch fine, but this would be my first night watch and I would be on deck all by myself. I was tired having not been able to sleep, but adrenalin soon took care of that.

Once above deck, after freshening up in the tiny head, Phyllis said, "Good evening! Are you ready?"

I nodded.

With that she briefed me with information I needed for my watch, "We want to keep on a heading of one-seventy. On the compass you want to keep it at about one-sixty-five. If on the GPS it gets much more than one-seventy-five or below one-sixty, then click off in the appropriate direction to correct our course." When the *Suena* was sailing – which it was at that moment – it had an automatic steering device – a wind-vane-like apparatus that adjusted the rudder according to wind direction. The wind-vane looked like a four-foot wing sticking out of the boat above the rudder in the back. If the adjustment got off – because of a change in the wind direction – then a simple "click" by pulling a cord on the mechanical device would adjust the wind-vane angle, and we would be back on course.

"We've been sailing at approximately five and a half knots," she continued, "with a cross current of about seven tenths. Not bad."

"If we get below three knots or if you have any questions – about course or making adjustments – or if you need help with anything at all, wake either Rick or I." She paused. I didn't say anything.

"No questions?"

"No," I said, "not right now."

"Coffee?"

"Sure."

Phyllis went below deck to put on the water.

I studied the GPS and compass. Then I used the flashlight to check the sail trim – there were small pieces of sail fabric like strings sown into the sail at various points, and they indicated how well wind was passing over that part of the sail. By checking these "trim tabs" one could tell if the sail was adjusted for optimum efficiency and power. It looked good. Then I moved around the boat just to get the feel of things, which was different at night. I also wanted to ask any questions while Phyllis was still awake. I was still a little nervous, but everything was in order. As the expression goes, it was smooth sailing: The sailboat was on course, no clouds, the stars were extremely clear, the wind was ideal, the sails were trimmed, the air was cool and fresh, and the sound of the water was soothing. Soon Phyllis came up with my coffee. She stayed on deck a few minutes making sure I was settled in, then said good-night and left me alone with the night.

Once alone I walked around the deck again to get an even better sense of my surroundings. Night on the sailboat had a completely different feeling than during the day, especially while we were sailing. It was like being in a different world. I needed to use up my nervous energy again – my first night watch – so moving around felt good. It didn't take me long to fall in love with the night on the *Suena*, above deck alone. The beauty of nature was unmistakable, and I felt safe on the *Suena*. It was the most comfortable solitude I had ever experienced! It was a feeling of contentment, beauty and mystery. It was also the perfect environment to contemplate life, be aware of the awesomeness of creation.

After a while I began to question whether or not my eyes were playing tricks on me: the water appeared to be glowing. At first I would catch a fleeting glimpse out of the corner of my eye of a glow that would almost simultaneously appear and disappear on the crest of a wave. Did I see something? I wondered. It definitely was not a reflection of the moon.

Then I noticed that the water close to the boat was glowing. The flow of water around the boat and the eddies it caused would fleetingly glow in streamers of pale, green light, like random flitings on a computer screen in a dark room. At closer inspection I could make out sparkles of light as far as six to eight feet below the surface of the water, directly beneath the boat. Flowing behind the boat was an almost violent display of the soft green glows in the turbulent wake of the *Suena* as she moved through the water. Obviously the movement of the *Suena* disrupting the smooth water was helping to precipitate the glow.

I recalled the first time I had seen phosphorescence in the sea. I was in the village of Melekeok, sitting halfway along a stone pier that extended about 150 yards from the shore. It was about 9:00 or 10:00 pm on a spectacularly clear night. I had an almost complete panorama of the starry sky, with no moon to obscure the stars, and before me was a stretch of shallow waters protected by the reef just beyond the pier.

I had been staring at the waters, lost in thought, when I began to notice fleeting glows of pale light in the water. My thoughts were pulled from their lofty heights to focus on these elusive glows. I tried to look at them, but it was like trying to watch lightning: you stare, waiting, and when it appears it is out of the corner of your eye, and when you focus your eyes on its origin the glow is already gone. Except phosphorescence is more frustrating because the glow is more subtle than lightning, leaving more questions of, *Did I see something or am I going crazy?*

About this time one of the boys from the village joined me, sitting next to me on the pier. As many boys of grade school age, he had a string of stories to relate to me, of no particular consequence, except to be shared. I enjoyed his company as I kept looking for the elusive phosphorescence.

While he was taking a breath between stories I asked, "Is the water glowing?" Without skipping a beat he said, "Oh, yes. That's phosphorescence." He continued his stream of words to explain that phosphorescence is produced by the plankton in the water. I asked him how to say phosphorescence in Palauan. He told me. I tried to repeat him. He corrected me and I tried again. This went on for a number of minutes until I could say it reasonably well, but by morning I could not remember the word.

As I watched the phosphorescence from the *Suena* I was fascinated, and it was much less frustrating than that night in Melekeok since the disruptions of the water caused by the boat elicited quite distinct glowings. They could be quite bright, even. I thought about how many organisms there were, mere feet from me, causing this mysterious light. I read that there can be upwards of 500 million organisms per one liter of water. That would mean only 10 liters of water – about five gallons – could hold a population of plankton organisms equivalent to the human population on the

Earth. I was not alone on that boat in the middle of the ocean! I wondered how many thousands produced each sparkle I saw in the water.

It's amazing to me that the largest animal on the Earth – the blue whale, a baleen whale – survives on plankton, the phytoplankton being the first link in the aquatic food chain; how does such a large creature – up to 200 tons – survive on microscopic organisms?

A blue whale calf weighing 1.8 metric tons at birth will double its weight in the first week; that's over 400 pounds of growth every day. That's a lot of plankton going to produce mother's milk.

I also find it fascinating to note that blue whales do most of their feeding on plankton blooms during the summer months in the polar seas. They then spend the winter in tropical zones, but often fast during this winter time. Odd how they feast in a seemingly lifeless place and fast in a place teeming with life. The glowing plankton I was seeing was safe from the appetite of the blue whale. But not the manta ray – the largest of the rays, also a plankton feeder.

We humans are more closely connected to the plankton than we realize. Certainly rain forests are more important to us than we can possibly fathom, but it's the plankton that produces an estimated 90% of free oxygen. It's good to occasionally remind myself how I am so connected – and dependent on – this vast and complicated planet I live on.

I was engrossed in these thoughts as I stared, mesmerized, at the soft, yet lively, glows surrounding the *Suena*. That first night watch went without event. I woke up Rick at 4:00 am and went below deck to lie on my couch. I was asleep in seconds.

I woke up early the next morning. I was still excited to be on a sailboat and out on the ocean. I went above deck. It was a beautiful day: the sun golden, the sky azure, a light sea breeze enough to sail by, very few clouds, the water smooth and blue with gentle swells. I greeted Phyllis and Rick and they had "good mornings" for me. I looked around and saw ocean all around – Palau was no longer in sight. I felt a few different things. First, I began to think about the fact that I could not see land in any direction. This was an odd feeling, but not enough to frighten me because the other feeling was stronger. I felt sadness at no longer being able to see Palau, realizing that Palau was now in my past, I could no longer even hold on to its sight.

After a few moments of greeting the morning I returned below deck to get myself breakfast and keep myself busy. I very soon began to realize the challenge of doing even simple things on a moving boat. I decided to have cereal and coffee – one of my favorite breakfasts. The seas were smooth, but the swells meant everything was constantly moving up and down, tilting this way and that, back and forth, plus there was the occasional odd wave giving the sailboat an extra jerk.

I leaned against the counter for stability and reached over the stove, unlatched and opened a compartment, and reached out a pan for water. Once I had pan in hand I held onto the sink with my other hand, held the pan under the facet, and pressed the foot pump (a small rubber "bump" on the floor), discharging water in the pan.

"Oops," I said to myself, as I realized I had been pressing the saltwater pump instead of the fresh water pump. I emptied the saltwater, put my food on the other pump, and pumped fresh water, first to rinse the pan, then to fill it for coffee water.

Pan with water, I put in on one of the propane burners. The seas were calm enough so I didn't need the pot clamps. I grabbed the spark-gun hanging on a hook, turned on the burner and sparked away. No flame. I tried again. Nothing. Then I realized the propane was off – one of Rick's cardinal rules. I stepped over to the propane valve and turned it twice. This time the burner ignited.

While the water heated I reached down a bowl from a side cupboard and a spoon from the utensil rack. I unlatched the lower cupboard and reached out a plastic container of cereal. While I was unscrewing the top, still leaning against the counter for stability and hands occupied, a swell tipped the *Suena* in the other direction which started containers sliding toward the open cabinet door. I slammed the cupboard door to prevent stuff from spilling out, almost falling over myself and spilling cheerios all over the floor. Later when I put the cereal container away I remembered there was a high lip on each shelf which would have prevented the containers from sliding out the door anyway. I cleaned up the spilled Cheerios as fast as I could, hoping Rick or Phyllis wouldn't see my bumbling.

Mess cleaned up I poured cereal in my bowl, secured the top on the cereal container, and returned it to its cupboard, closed and latched it. I got an individual milk out of the ice box, picked up my bowl and walked – unsteadily and slowly – to the table. I put the bowl and carton on the table, and was returning to the galley for my coffee when I saw the bowl sliding toward the edge of the table. Cheerios all over the floor a second time. "This won't do," I said to myself as I picked up Cheerios again. I put the bowl (with salvaged Cheerios) on the couch, in the corner, and placed a pillow to hold it in place.

By this time the water was boiling.

Back at the galley I got out the instant coffee and put some in a cup – a wide bottomed cup to help prevent tipping (but not sliding). I put the top back on the coffee jar before trying to pour the hot water in the cup. When the coffee was stirred and everything was back in place, I was ready to begin breakfast!

I was making my way back to the table – carefully with a hot cup of coffee in my hand – when I remembered I had to turn off the propane. Don't ever forget to turn off the propane!

When all was secured I could finally enjoy my breakfast in peace.

I went on my second day-watch at noon. The first thing was to complete my new, and essential, beginning-watch-ritual; cover every exposed part of my body with sunscreen -- the sun was relentless, and I knew starting out with a sunburn would not be good. I don't tan, and who would I impress with one anyway?

Rick was below deck reading or sleeping. Phyllis talked with me some before going below deck herself. The solitude was nice. The sun was intense, but if I stayed in the shade of the cockpit canopy I was fine. I had a book with me, but I found myself still too concerned about watching sails, bearing, and horizon to relax enough to enjoy reading. We were under sail, but just barely – the wind was light.

Before the end of my watch I had to wake Rick from a nap because the wind had become so weak. He saw our wind speed on the GPS and sighed, his brow furrowed. He moaned to himself and said to no one in particular, "We'll have to start the engine." Rick knew we'd probably have to use the engine some during the trip but he was disappointed it had happened so early.

Phyllis came above deck and squatted to manipulate a small handle near the floor of the cockpit. Rick went down the steps where the ignition was located. "First be sure the engine is disengaged," Phyllis instructed, showing me the handle and button positions. She continued, "Find neutral, then push it forward about halfway." She did as she said, then called to Rick, "0kay!" Rick pushed the ignition button and the engine roared to life.

"Now," Phyllis said, "we wait five minutes before engaging. Then run at twenty to twenty-five thousand rpm – the tachometer is just down the steps." A simple procedure, but being new to me it was jumbled in my head. But I had to remember; later in the trip I would have to do it all on my own.

The engine was loud and smelled, which wasn't pleasant, but it kept us moving at a reasonable pace – about four or five knots. We left up the mainsail (which always stays up) and jib. There was still some wind, which was giving us an extra knot or two, so we were "motor sailing," as Rick called it.

It was Phyllis' turn to cook, and when she had dinner prepared Rick turned off the motor. There was very little wind, but it did keep us moving, albeit, very slowly. It was nice, however, to eat without the noise and smell of the engine.

After drinks and sunset – again, very spectacular – we were barely moving, so the engine was fired up again.

I went below deck and read for about an hour using the battery powered lamps before attempting to sleep before my watch. I slept fitfully. Phyllis woke me up five minutes before midnight. I changed my clothes, washed my face, used the head, and got a drink of water before going up. Phyllis reminded me of my duties and the bearing I should keep for the night. After a few minutes she was satisfied that I was set and she went below deck. The engine was still going, so I had to steer manually, which I found was most easily done while standing.

While sailing, the automatic wind-vane steering system kept us on course. The person on watch just periodically checked course on the GPS and compass and made infrequent adjustments. It was very possible to get a lot of reading done when the boat was sailing. Manual steering, however, required constant attention. One had to choose a point in the distance to steer toward, like a building, a mountain, or, while in the middle of an ocean, a cloud. It didn't take long to realize that at night the stars are the best help in navigating.

A few months before leaving for Palau I took my then present students to a planetarium for science class. To my surprise and joy, the show was about how Micronesian seafarers used the stars to navigate through the pacific. It was eerie how the subject of this show seemed to be tailored just for me; I was interested in sailing and I was about to go to Micronesia (of which Palau is a part). Sailing on a traditional canoe has become another dream of mine.

I began to read about it, which only peaked my interest more. Through my reading I discovered that the Micronesian island of Satawal – considered an outer island of Yap – had some of the best known traditional navigators. In fact the Carolinians who live on Saipan most likely came from the islands in the region of Satawal. One of the last navigators – for unfortunately the art seems to be dieing out – was Mau Pialug. He has been mentioned in a number of books, including The Last Navigator by Steven Thomas and The Hokule'a: The Way to Tahiti by Ben Finney. He is a legend and I was honored to meet him in Palau. There was a commemoration for the Yapese Navigators who mined Yapese money from Palau. He was on the island of Oolong (near where we anchored the *Suena* that very first night) for a ceremony. I saw him from afar. He looked pensive. I made my way closer to him, but I was embarrassed to approach him, because who was I? Finally I introduced myself and we had a short conversation. He gave me no big secrets, nor did I ask for any, but it was nice to at least shake his hand and tell him I admired his talent.

A few years after my voyage on the *Suena* I had the opportunity to at least partially realize my dream of sailing on a traditional canoe. I would have liked to have sailed from one Micronesian island to another. Not quite possible, but I did get a ride on a Satawalese canoe in Saipan. It was a ride about a mile out toward Managha, and then back. Short, but for me it was awesome!

Using the tiller to steer the *Suena*, it didn't take a stretch of the imagination to realize why ancient mariners knew so much about the stars. I checked the compass frequently, but I found the stars could keep the boat almost perfectly on course without the compass. There were so many stars to choose from! It was just a matter of choosing the right one. It was fascinating, and it gave me an opportunity to become more familiar with the night sky which had fascinated me since childhood. It wasn't as enjoyable to use the engine as it was to sail, but even steering the night watch was a special time. There was something about being on a sailboat at night in the middle of the ocean and under the stars, that filled me with awe. It was a very comfortable feeling. Of all the things about sailing, the night watch was never a disappointment, but rather always a high point of the day which lifted any dampened spirits.

I was enjoying the night, the ocean, the solitude, the stars, the moon, the mystery, the sound of the water rushing past the boat. I was also feeling more and more comfortable with the boat; I wasn't so nervous and I was much more relaxed. I didn't have to check the compass quite as often and I learned to scan the horizon with less effort. Steering was a constant job, but even that was less of a chore with some practice (which I got a lot of on a four-hour watch). Steering manually forced me to become more familiar with the constellations. Rick had helped me with some of the names of individual stars and I tried to memorize as many as possible. I brought a star book up from below deck to help me with this task. Periodically I would steal a look through the binoculars – incredible! So many stars! And all those points of light in the sky are not all just stars: globular clusters, planets, galaxies. We live in such an interesting universe. I didn't have names for all the constellations, so until I learned the proper names I made up my own. Such a beautiful night sky! Why do we so seldom notice it?

The night wore on but my awe didn't wane. I was exceptionally aware of my surroundings: the waves, the sounds of the boat, the smell of the air, the stars, the horizon, the bearing and GPS readings. It was about 2:30 am when I noticed that the wind was increasing. Slightly, but it was increasing. Soon my thought was, *Is it strong enough to sail on?* It was hard to tell with my inexperience; the wind was stronger, certainly, but it wasn't an obviously powerful wind. So I was left with the question: *Should I shut down the engine and sail, adjusting the sails on my own?* I had not yet done on my own, so I wondered, should I wait until it was Rick's watch and let him make the decision and make the adjustments? This was the easy – and safe – thing to do.

But something inside nagged me. I felt a pressure to do it on my own, to take the chance of doing it wrong, to be brave enough to try. The longer I waited the more pressure I felt to shut down the engine and try to sail on my own. My palms became sweaty. My heart rate was increasing. I went to the front of the boat a number of times to check out the jib and its trim tabs and it seemed suitable for sailing, but I wanted to be convinced. All the indicators pointed to sailing, and checking the jib gave me confidence. When I got back to the tiller, however, the boat was way off course. I could get on course easy enough, but this meant that when I checked the jib the angle of the sails to the wind was different, making my evaluation of the jib trim questionable. This evaporated my confidence. Then there was the problem of getting the wind-vane steering apparatus up and working properly.

Finally I decided I just couldn't wait for Rick's watch – there was still an hour on my watch – and I knew for my own peace of mind I had to try. I took a few deep breaths and ran through my mind what I was going to do. I got the steering apparatus ready to hook up. I got the boat on course and trimmed the sails as best I could. Then I idled the engine and put it in neutral. I hooked the steering apparatus chain to the rudder – which was more difficult and took longer than I had first thought. I had to manually steer the rudder to get the boat on course before I could comfortably let the steering apparatus do the work. I checked the sails again. I could adjust the sails from the cockpit using the sheets, checking the inside trim using a flashlight from the cockpit to see the inside trim-tails.

Then, everything was set – as much as I could do from the cockpit -- and we were sailing. We were sailing! And the speed indicator said we were going fast enough not to need the engine. I had done it!

But before I turned off the engine (I would have to wake Rick to turn it on again, so I wanted to make sure everything was set before doing that final step) I had to check the outside jib trim. This was not quite as easy because I could not do it from the cockpit. I must note here that I was not using safety lines. The reason being that the waves were not that big, nor the seas choppy nor rough. Rick did warn me, however, that should I fall off the boat – even if he and/or Phyllis were on deck – that I should just consider myself dead. This was because it was almost impossible to find a man overboard because of the vastness of the ocean and the fact that the swells help to hide a person in the water. At night alone… I perished the thought. But with the ocean so calm I didn't see the necessity. I would be careful, I promised myself.

So anyway… to check the outside trim I had to go to the prow of the *Suena*, hold on while I was leaning over the railing, and shine the flashlight up to see the trim tails on the outside of the sail, seawater splashing on me as the hull of the boat plunged into the down side of the swells. Then I would rush back, relatively speaking, to the cockpit and adjust the sheets, then hurry back to the prow to check if my adjustments were an improvement. It took me about fifteen minutes to be satisfied with the trim of the sails.

It was time to turn off the engine. I took a deep breath, revved the engine – as instructed – and shut it off. The resulting quiet was music to my ears – just the sounds of wind and water. Much better than the assault of the engine. We were on course and sailing at five knots. I felt so good inside – I got the boat sailing on my very own! I was filled with positive energy. Smooth sailing!

But it didn't end there because another question popped into my mind (although not as insistent), *Should I put up the staysail?* The wind seemed to have increased a bit more, but enough to put up the staysail? I again had to go through an internal struggle. Could I do it? This meant putting up a sail, not just trimming a sail that was already up. I was surging with energy and my confidence was boosted.

I checked the course, the speed, and the trim. I went forward to the staysail. I untied the halyard and raised the staysail as rapidly and quietly – an impossibility on a steel-hull boat – as possible. I wrapped the halyard around the winch four times, as Rick had instructed, hoping I did it in the right direction, then cranked it tight. I hurried back to the cockpit and trimmed the staysail. I did it again! I was elated the rest of my watch.

This was the time I really wanted to talk to Pilordes, share me excitement. My excitement was similar to when we would occasionally go to lunch in Palau. If I had some extra time during lunch – not often – I would tell her and we would try to meet for lunch. We would go to different places, always near the ocean: the K-B bridge, T-dock, Malakal Park, Long-Island.

"I'll bring lunch," she would say, "you bring drinks and desert."

I would usually borrow a car from the Catholic Mission to pick her up at her residence. We would drive to one of our spots and have a feast. This usually meant rice and a can of tuna or corned beef. A side treat would be a small package of kimchee, which was mostly pickled taquan. For drinks and desert I would bring a can of Coke, a can of Dr. Pepper, and a package of M&Ms. Simple, but it always tasted so good! Good food, good views and great conversation. I longed for one of our great conversations at that moment.

I woke Rick up at 4:00 am. The moon was just dipping into the western horizon, casting a sparkling sheen on the water. When Rick came above deck I told him I turned off the engine because the wind picked up, and then put up the staysail. I told him I wasn't sure if it was trimmed right, but I did the best I could. He grunted, acknowledging my message. I went below deck and was able to fall quickly into a satisfied sleep.

When I awoke the next day I looked around and I was at home. I had only been on the sailboat for three days. Not a long time, but living on a sailboat is an intimate experience which makes three days a long time, enough time to become a part of the surrounding, to make this place my home.

I enjoyed my breakfast of cereal with cold milk while I read (I saved the coffee until later). Afterwards I went above deck to say hello to Rick and Phyllis and catch a glimpse of the beautiful surroundings! I hung around for a few minutes breathing in the sea air, observing the weather and waves, saying "good-morning" to the sea, sun, sky, and *Suena*, then went back below deck to read and nap before my watch in a few hours. I got restless and went above deck about an hour early. It was a very beautiful day as the days had been. I went through my daily, essential ritual of smearing my body with sunscreen.

I had been above deck for about ten or fifteen minutes, just hanging out with Rick and Phyllis, enjoying the sailing, when Phyllis said excitedly with a smile, "Did Rick tell you?"

I furrowed my brow, questioning, indicating I hadn't heard. Phyllis said, "You put up and adjusted the sails perfect last night!"

"Oh?" I said.

"You did a very good job!" Phyllis said.

"Oh," I said, "I didn't know." Outward I was nonchalant, but inward I was full of pride.

Phyllis said to Rick, who was there but looking out toward the horizon, "He did a good job didn't he, Rick."

He reluctantly grunted an acknowledgement.

"I'm glad I'm learning," I said meekly. I was very appreciative to Phyllis for sharing my triumph. I was, however, curious why Rick didn't say anything himself. At least he acknowledged my achievement, even if his acknowledgment was oblique and seemed forced. I knew I had succeeded and had made an important step in my sailing education.

My day watch that day went fine, although we were sailing very slow, right on the brink of needing the engine. It seemed like a long watch. The ocean was beautiful as always, but the sun was bright and hot, and there was so little breeze that the heat felt stagnant. The turtle pace of the boat dampened my spirits a bit. I passed the time by reading. I was finishing Malcolm X, a good book and welcome stimulation. However, I was beginning to miss a long walk. I knew it was going to be a long trip, and already we were traveling slower than expected. I knew, however, that ten days wouldn't be too bad, and I could even handle two weeks, especially since part of the time was already over. To help out, I began to mentally divide the trip into legs, the first being from Koror to Helen's Reef – one of the most southern islands within the political governance of Palau.

After my watch it was my turn to cook dinner. I was nervous about cooking – I could barely get together cold cereal and instant coffee. But Rick and Phyllis had a menu planned for me and gave me a recipe to use. It turned out to be easy to cook once I got past my own doubts. The motion of the boat wasn't too severe, but even in the gentle water and relatively small swells cooking was very different than cooking in a conventional kitchen where everything stays where you put it, where you don't have to constantly hold everything, or clamp down the pots on the stove. It was an interesting challenge. But most important, the outcome was edible.

Dinner and sunset drinks were a very enjoyable time as they had been the previous days. A special time. A beautiful time. A peaceful and relaxing time. It was also a time for Rick, Phyllis and I to get to know each other better. We had some very interesting conversations on everything from religion and politics to our own personal histories.

The wind was dying on us, so after the sun had been down for awhile and we were all finished with our drinks, Rick started up the engine again. I hated to have the engine roaring, but not moving was worse. It was odd that we were using the engine so much, and we hadn't even reached the doldrums.

I was irritated at the slow pace, yet using an engine on a sailboat now seems to me almost like cheating. Have I been afflicted with the malady of our fast paced society? Everything today seems to say, "Have an experience already! Get something done! Accomplish something! And do it now!" Sailing should be all about countering that mentality. I recently read about some northern expeditions where ships would get stuck in arctic ice for a whole winter, sometimes two. Cold, little food, no sun for months! And I, on a comfortable boat stocked with food in beautiful weather, was irritated about traveling at less than three knots!

The next couple of days were about the same. I had developed a routine: Get up at 9:00 or 10:00 am, go above deck to greet the day (and Phyllis and Rick), eat cereal with cold milk (while it lasted), have some coffee and read until it was almost my watch at noon, go above deck a bit early to talk with Phyllis, do my four-hour watch, lay down for awhile and read, get up to eat and/or cook, have an evening drink above deck with Rick and Phyllis, enjoy the sunset, do dishes (if I didn't cook), do my daily meditation, read, try to get some sleep before my midnight watch, do my midnight watch (the part of the day I looked forward to), then start all over again. It was an easy routine, no complaints, really. However, I was starting to feel just a bit cramped on the sailboat after those few days. I was also missing Palau. And Pilordes. The day watches seemed especially long.

I was getting along well enough with Rick and Phyllis. Phyllis was very easy to be with and we had some good conversations. Rick was not a very good conversationalist, although there were brief moments during dinner and drinks when he added to the conversation.

"Are you religious?" he asked quite bluntly one evening.

I hesitated a moment before answering, "I would say I'm spiritual rather than religious."

Rick raised his eyebrows, nodding. "You're Catholic, right?"

"Yes."

"So you believe that if you aren't Catholic you're going to hell." It sounded like an accusation.

"No," I said, calmly. "I don't believe that, and the official Church does not teach that either. I believe – and this is my own opinion – that the important thing is to have a relationship with God. For me that is largely being aware of God's presence. The Catholic Church helps me in that; if it didn't help me I would cease being a Catholic. But many people, I believe, can and are, aware of the presence of the holy all around them, of the presence of God, whether or not they are Catholic. Or Christian. Or whatever religion, for that matter."

Rick nodded, but in a way that seemed to say, "To each his own." Phyllis didn't say anything, but she appeared interested.

The conversation continued and although he never criticized my viewpoint verbally, Rick had a way of showing contempt. I also noticed that he didn't praise anything I did, whether I did it well or not. But he was quick to point out my mistakes. At least things weren't tense or uncomfortable.

I began reading a book Phyllis recommended about a woman unjustly imprisoned in a Russian prison for eighteen years, so when I felt cramped I just had to think about that woman which put my situation in perspective. And still does today. But I was looking forward to reaching the end of our first leg of the journey – Helen's Reef. We would be there in a day or two.

Of the five islands of the Southwest Islands of Palau, they were divided into two Palauan States. I had set foot in fourteen of the sixteen states of Palau, the exceptions being Ngardmau and Helen's Reef/Tobi islands. I would at least get the chance to set foot in Helen's before I left Palau, but mostly I was looking forward to setting foot on Palauan soil again. I knew there would be some people there, and it would be nice to talk to a Palauan… one more time.

Helen's Reef is a reef about four to five miles in diameter, with a very small island on the northern part of the reef. The map also shows a number of shipwrecks.

Rick said we were getting close, but we wouldn't see it until we were very close – the only thing that really shows are the waves crashing on the reef, which can't be seen from very far off. Thus the shipwrecks; the reef often isn't seen until it's too late.

We were having a good wind – finally – as we got closer to Helen's Reef. Rick asked us to keep a lookout for the reef, but he suggested we also listen; we would probably hear the crashing waves on the reef before we would see them, and with the engine not going we should be able to hear the roar.

The waters were a little rougher than we had experienced up to this point, but the winds were better too. We had our usual drink at sunset, as we listened for the reef, but we weren't there quite yet.

When we finally heard the roar of the reef it was about an hour after sundown. Being too dark to risk sailing up the narrow passage in the reef to the small island, we hove to. I didn't quite understand the whole concept of heaving to, but I trusted that Rick knew what he was doing. Without anchoring he set the sails to hold us basically stationary, however we were drifting very slowly toward the reef. We hove to a number of miles from the reef so we would have plenty of room to spare. During my watch I just had to watch the GPS position, and if we got too close to the reef, I was to wake Rick and he would help me adjust our position.

About an hour into my watch the GPS showed that we were getting too close, and I could distinctly hear the roar. I hated to wake Rick, but it had to be done.

He didn't say anything – just a few grunts – as he evaluated our situation. After a few minutes he had decided where to move the sailboat. There was still good wind, so together we got it under sail. This was the type of experience I had come for. With the wind blowing Rick and I had to yell instructions and replies to each other. The waves were large enough to give the sailboat quite a bit of motion, water splashing over the bow. I went forward, keeping a hand tight on whatever stay was close, and raised the jib. The wind was ripping at the luff until I could get it all the way raised and Rick could pull in the sheet.

Once the sails were set and we were moving in the proper direction Rick told me what direction to steer the boat, but he told me I had to steer manually.

For the next two hours I steered the *Suena* through some fairly rough water. I put on Rick's raincoat because the night wind and water were cold. It was more difficult to navigate by the stars as they jumped up and down with the boat's motion, but they were bright and easy to see. It was much more tiring to steer manually, especially in the rougher waters, but it was much more exciting too. It made time pass quickly, and as far as I was concerned, sailing was great!

When the GPS indicated that we had reached our destination I again woke Rick and we hove to again. The rest of my watch I spent just waiting.

In the morning I went to sleep, but could only sleep for a few hours – waiting for the sun to come up. Rick wanted all hands on deck for making the narrow passage through the reef to the tiny island. And, besides, I couldn't sleep as we approached Helen's Island! I had always wanted to go to Helen's, and there I finally was.

Chapter 3

Helen's Reef

The day was gorgeous; the sun was out, sky deep blue, few clouds in the sky. We had a good wind and were under sail.

Up on deck the white of the waves could easily be seen crashing on Helen's Reef. Outside the reef the water was a deep blue, inside the reef the colors of the water were a spectrum of pale blues and greens, although the reflections of the low sun made it difficult to make out the colors.

We were sailing, approaching the reef from the northwest and we would parallel the reef on the west side to reach the channel through the west reef. We were sailing relatively slow because Rick didn't want to attempt the narrow channel until the sun was higher, reducing the glare, making it easier to see dangerous, extraneous reef. We had plenty of time to get to the channel.

The small island – Helen's Island – was visible on the north rim of the huge reef enclosure. Almost invisible against the horizon, it was low with little vegetation, and the only things that set it off (through binoculars) were a flag pole flying an American flag, a cluster of three short palms, and one lone, tall palm tree. We knew from Mike at the State Office in Koror there would be two people on the island and they should be expecting us.

My excitement settled as the *Suena* leisurely skirted the beautiful reef. At our relaxed speed it took a few hours to reach the channel, the small island receding to the north.

As we neared the opening of the channel we saw a speed boat come from the direction of Helen's Island, also paralleling the reef, but on the other side. There were three men in the boat; we wondered who the extra man was. They were obviously checking us out. We waved and they returned the greeting, but we were too far to hear or be heard. They watched us for awhile then seemed to lose interest and headed southeast to another part of the large reef becoming a dot in the distance, then disappearing along the sky-ocean horizon. We leisurely continued toward the channel.

My excitement began to rise again when we could visually make out the break in the reef. Adrenalin began to fill our bodies and Rick began to give us instructions to get ready. He explained to us how we would do our approach to the opening and the plan for navigating the channel. I heard the edge creep into Rick's voice and I saw his body tense up. I knew the harsh tone and hard words were soon to follow.

Rick had been studying the map. It was an unfamiliar passage for him, and he didn't completely trust the map, so he was nervous. Now it was time. We took our positions: Rick at the prow to do the navigating with his chart, compass, and experience, Phyllis on the rudder, and I on the sheets.

"This isn't going to be easy," Rick said. "We are going to have to tack, and there's not much room to tack in."

He continued with a loud voice, "When I say turn, turn the tiller to the east, at eighty degrees."

Both Phyllis and I were very attentive; I still wanted to do everything just right, and I had no desire to incite the captain's wrath. Somehow, though, that seemed impossible.

"I said," Rick yelled with a harsh tone, "to turn the boat on course of eighty degrees when I say!"

"Okay Rick," Phyllis said with a combination of anger and hurt.

"Phyllis," Rick said in a tone of voice that seemed to contain something bordering on hate, "you must respond to everything… everything! I need to know you heard me."

"Okay, Rick," she said in her same tone of voice. "I'm sorry," she added with a tone of hopelessness.

"I'm not mad at you," Rick said in a gentler tone, yet filled with frustration, "but I need to know you've heard all my commands, otherwise we'll end up on the reef."

"Yes, Rick, I know," Phyllis complained, "but you don't need to shout."

Rick sighted audibly with contempt, but said with obvious forced calm, "I'm not shouting because I'm angry, I'm shouting because I need to be heard clearly."

Phyllis began to tell Rick that his tone of voice was offensive, and began to distinguish between a shout and yell. Rick was about to get into it with her. I was feeling uncomfortable because of the tension between them, and the channel was nearing rapidly. Finally Rick said, "I would love to discuss it, but we'll have to save it for later."

A few moments later he said "Now!" and Phyllis turned the boat in the direction Rick indicated. After the turn he yelled "More left!" Phyllis complied, but Rick yelled, "I said, 'more left!'"

"I'm sorry, Rick!" she shot back. "I turned left," she said and steered the boat even more. Rick grumbled as we sailed on.

"Okay," Rick said, "We're going to do a tack to starboard. But we won't stay that course for very long, then we'll do a tack to port. Okay?"

"Okay," Phyllis replied. I didn't say anything. He turned and asked in a harsh tone if I had heard. I realized I had just made the same mistake as Phyllis.

"Yes," I answered.

"I need to hear a reply to every command," he scolded me. His scoldings were really annoying, but I didn't show my aggravation.

He gave Phyllis instructions on bearing and me instructions on the tack, then he asked, "Are you ready?" Phyllis said, "Ready." For some reason I didn't say anything. He scolded me again, "I need an answer to every command!"

"Ready!" I said loudly.

We glided along, Rick studying the water. Then he yelled, "Steer to three-fifty!"

Phyllis replied, "Three-fifty!"

Rick yelled, "Tack!"

I began to release the starboard jib-sheet. Rick yelled again, with anger, "Tack!"

Phyllis replied for me, "Tacking!"

Rick yelled, "Every command! Every command!"

I realized I had made the same mistake twice in less than a minute. I scolded myself this time!

When I saw there would be no override on the sheet I jumped to the port sheet and began hauling it in, and when it got tight I used the hand crank on the winch. Phyllis helped by taking care of the excess rope.

"More!" Rick screamed, and I strained my muscles to get another two cranks in before he said, "Okay."

"Okay!" I echoed.

Phyllis said quietly, "That's right, echo everything he says." I could see the importance of the feedback, but Rick's manner stung. But what option did I have?

It was a fairly long channel, and especially hard to tack through. It took two or three hours to get to within a quarter mile of Helen's Island. It went smoothly, however. We learned to work as a team, especially Phyllis and I, and we got our tasks down pat. Even so, Rick continued to let his tension get the best of him, and consequently Phyllis and I were scolded a lot – Phyllis much more often and more mercilessly than I.

We were there. Helen's Island! I was excited to get ashore. I had been at sea only five days, but it seemed like a very long time, and I longed to step on solid ground again. And I was ready to be free of the tension that was building on the boat. I found myself angry at Rick – his tone was out of line. I was angry for both myself and Phyllis. I wanted a long walk to dissipate my emotions. Anything more than 36 feet would have been nice.

We had been through the most dangerous part of the channel and were approaching the island when the speed boat approached us, coming alongside the *Suena*. They tied up and two of the three men boarded our boat. "Hello!" Rick said with a large, enthusiastic smile. "Welcome aboard the *Suena!*" Rick shook each man's hand vigorously. Then Phyllis and I did the same.

The first man said his name was Max. He spoke first and with authority. He had on dark sunglasses and was wearing a new baseball-style cap that said "POLICE" on the front. I recognized it as the same style the policemen wore in Koror. I wondered if a friend had given him the cap. He had on a smart looking T-shirt covered with a nice looking khaki shirt. He was a small man, but appeared solid and muscular. He had the facial features of a Southwest Islander. He smiled broadly when he shook our hands.

The other man introduced himself as Franno. He also had Southwest features, but was not at all athletic looking. Franno appeared soft and slightly chubby. He wore no hat or sunglasses, and his T-shirt looked comfortably worn. He had a happy-go-lucky smile that emanated from inside.

"We were expecting you," Max said.

"We would have been here earlier," Rick spoke slowly and deliberately, "but very little wind." He shrugged his shoulders dramatically with his hands spread.

"Would you like coffee?" Phyllis asked. "Yes," they both said.

"What about him?" Rick asked, indicating the man still in the boat.

Max said, "He is the captain of an Indonesian fishing boat. He and his crew are fishing here. They have a license from Helen's Reef/Tobi state Government to fish for sea cucumbers."

"Invite him up!" Rick said with exaggerated excitement.

Max talked to the captain in Indonesian and the man climbed aboard.

Rick said, "Salamat siang!"

The Indonesian replied, "Salamat siang." Everyone sat down at Rick's invitation.

"Did you have a good trip," Max asked.

Rick responded, "Yes, but, like I said before, little wind. But very smooth." He continued speaking as if to a child, using his hands in a sign language that also appeared more suitable for children.

"You both live here?" Rick asked in the same belittling tone, pointing to the small island off the port beam.

"Yes," Max said with pride. "I am the policeman, and Franno is the radioman." That would explain the cap, I thought to myself.

Franno grinned from ear to ear. "We protect our reef from poachers,"

Max continued explaining, "We both are from the island of Tobi." Tobi is also part of the Southwest islands and is a small island, but not nearly as small as Helen's. Tobi was about 50 miles distant further south and west from where we were. "He's from Indonesia," Max said pointing the third man sipping coffee quietly, smiling.

We all sat there drinking our coffee in the early afternoon sun, chatting, mostly Rick asking questions. Both of the Palauan men began to fidget. Finally Max asked seriously, "Did you bring anything from the state Office?"

"Oh, yes," Rick said, and dispatched me to get it.

I brought back a sack of rice, some buckets, and a box. Instead of waiting to get back to their island, they began to immediately open the box. Not seeing what they were looking for on the top of the package, they rummaged deeper.

"Ah," Max said with relief and a smile. He reached deep in the box and pulled out a carton of cigarettes. Big smiles spread on the faces of Franno and the Indonesian.

"You're out of cigarettes," Rick said and laughed genially.

"No," Max corrected. "We still have these." He pulled out of his pocket some Indonesian clove cigarettes. He added, "But we want American cigarettes."

All three men lit up cigarettes and breathed sighs of relief. Then Franno pulled out a small bag and began to dig out some betelnut. I had seen a lot of this in Palau.

"Ka molamech?" I asked.

"Chochoi. E kau?"

"Choi."

"Soam a molamech?"

"Choi. Soak."

"Ka molekoi a tekoi a Belau ma ungil," Max commented.

"Ng diak," I said and smiled at the compliment. Franno handed me the small bag and I fixed a betelnut for myself to chew. Max and Franno smiled at me. I felt I had made a connection with the two Palauans.

The three men retuned to Helen's Island while we found a good spot to anchor the *Suena*. Inside the reef the water was very calm, almost like glass. After five days of ocean swells the stableness of the boat felt like a luxury. I took the opportunity to straighten up my cabinet space a bit and then I went for a nice swim.

The water was beautiful! After all, it was still Palauan water: it had the colors, the smell, the feel. It felt good to be there, I knew I was still in Palau and I felt at home. I was excited to go ashore and be with Franno and Max.

It was also a time for a freshwater shower. We had to conserve our fresh water – we had plenty, but fresh water is a matter of life and death, something to be conserved at sea, even when there seems to be plenty. Showers weren't necessary on the sailboat, and I got used to not showering, but instead used a soapy rag. Taking a bucket shower, with seawater, and rinsing with fresh water was a luxury. Finally that salty stickiness washed away.

It was about three in the afternoon when we boarded the dingy and went ashore. I wanted to stay the night on the island, so I brought with me the things I would need, just in case.

Going ashore the water was beautiful. I had my camera with me so I took a number of pictures of Helen's Island; this was a once in a lifetime experience, and it was a beautiful sight. There were also a number of large clouds in the northern sky that looked like they would bring rain. We anchored the dingy fifty yards from shore and we waded inland. It felt so good for my feet to sink into the sand, feel the cool water around my ankles.

We stepped on the island in the middle of the south side. The Palauan's "settlement" was in the middle of the north side. We crossed the island and found Max working on a cabinet. Franno was looking on, speaking to Max in Sonsoralese (their native language). The Indonesian captain was trying to help Max, talking to him in Indonesian. Franno and Max greeted us in· English and continued working on the cabinet. They chatted with me in Palauan. They spoke comfortably in all four languages, and had no trouble switching from one language to the other.

Rick began talking to them. I wanted to be away from Rick, and I couldn't wait for Rick and Phyllis to go back to the *Suena*. I wanted to ask either Franno or Max if I could stay the night on the island, but it wasn't the right time. So I went for a walk to the end of the island.

Helen's Island is a small island, even by island standards. I estimated it was about two-hundred yards long (east-west) and fifty yards wide (north-south). It was covered with a vegetation that seemed to be cross between a bush and a tree; they were low – about fifteen feet tall – and airy, yet provided essential shade. There were the four coconut trees on the island that we saw through the binoculars, but not much else in terms of vegetation.

A distinguishing feature of Helen's Island was its birds. There were thousands of them that lived on the west end. Terns and boobys. Mostly terns; a few different species. Terns live in many parts of the world, but mostly in subtropical and tropical regions, like Palau. Terns have short legs, straight sharp bills, narrow wings, and forked tails. I estimated the wingspan of these terns at two to two and a half feet. To me the terns looked to be very sleek and dexterous fliers. Standing on the beach and looking up, the sky was in motion with hundreds, maybe thousands, of birds. I always wondered if birds' wings got tired after flying for long periods of time. I would especially think about this when we were far out to sea, no land in sight, seeing birds fly by. How can these birds fly so far and long? I wondered. Don't they need to sleep, or at least rest? I found out later that many terns migrate long distances, one species, the arctic tern, migrates from the far north to the Antarctic region. I didn't know if this was non-stop, but when I read on I guessed it was. The young of the sooty tern don't breed until they are about three years old, some staying in the air this whole time – three years! For these terns does it feel like a rest when they finally land to raise a family, or is it that they can't avoid it because their wings finally got tired and they had to land?

When I walked to the west end of the small island there were hundreds and hundreds of these birds on the ground. The sound they made was constant and loud, but it blended in with, and complimented, the roar of the surf.

To the north of the island the waves crashed on the reef about one-hundred yards away. The reef extended east and west and curved around to meet five miles south of Helen's Island. From the island at least three ships – large ones, at least one hundred feet each – could be clearly seen wrecked on the reef.

As I looked around I felt privileged to be in a place that very few have had the opportunity to be, and it was good to be on Palauan soil, even though it was so far from where I was used to.

It was a short walk, but it was so nice to walk! To stand in the shade of a tree, to be more than 36 feet away from other humans! I watched the birds, waded in the water, picked up some seashells, reflected on my experience and the beauty of this remote, unique and special place.

When I got back to the others I sat nearby quietly and studied my surroundings. We were gathered in a work area: a large shed with a large tin awning extending over some tables and benches. Another, smaller, shed was just to the east, and there were three very dilapidated, obviously unused buildings to the southeast. I had heard that eight people lived on Helen's Island at one time. These must have been their homes. To the west was a small building that was new and I guessed was a house for Franno or Max, or both. There wasn't much else. A bird was in a cage hanging on a low branch, and a booby – a large, dirty white bird with webbed feet – was tied to a tree. A small garden with a wire fence around it was under the bush-trees to the south. There was a water tank to the south of the newer looking house with gutters connected to the house. A solar panel was mounted on a tall pole above the house with a cable snaking down and disappearing under the eaves. A tall flagpole stood in the middle of it all.

Rick was "helping" Max with the cabinet. In fact, Rick was telling Max how to do just about everything, but Rick was doing nothing himself. I couldn't understand how Rick could fail to see Max's irritation, or that Max was doing just fine on his own.

When Rick tired of helping Max, who had stopped responding to Rick but was somehow tolerating him, Rick promised to bring some sandpaper back from the *Suena*. Rick had used up all the Indonesian words he knew on the captain, who was looking flustered. Rick then noticed a tank of diesel fuel and asked Franno about it. They had no use for it so Rick offered to buy it (we had already used more gas than we had expected). While Franno and Rick were agreeing on a price I asked Max if it would be all right if I could stay the night on Helen's. He said, "Of course." It turned out that the next day was my birthday, and I couldn't think of anything better than to wake up on my birthday on Helen's Island! Max smiled and said I was welcome to think of this as my home, especially since I was a Palauan. I was very flattered with this compliment, and I felt his hospitality to be sincere.

Negotiations finished, I was glad to help Rick drag the diesel tank to the water where Rick floated it back to the *Suena*. I felt so free seeing Rick and Phyllis go back to the sailboat without me. Standing on Helen's Island I felt like I was at home. I felt buoyant being off the sailboat and on Palau again.

But I was also tired from lack of sleep and a busy morning and afternoon, so I asked Max if there was a place I could take a nap. Max led me to the shack just north of the "work" shack. He said this was where the Indonesian captain slept, but it would be okay for me to take a nap there.

It was definitely a shack. It was made from warped two-by-fours and peeling plywood that must have been quite old. The floor was sand with a number of inverted cones in the sand – evidence of ant-lions. The wooden shutters on the "windows" were propped open (no glass, of course). There were no doors on either of the two doorways. There were platforms along both walls, extending from door to door. Nets hung from the ceiling and more were piled on the platforms, leaving just enough space for an old, thin, vinyl mattress. No pillow, so I used my daypack, which I had with me. I laid down in this simple abode. It was so simple, but it didn't need to be anymore elaborate. Being only four degrees north of the equator the storms were mild, and being in a tropical region surrounded by ocean the climate was always – day, night, all year 'round – temperate. No need for heat, no need for A.C. A few pieces of wood pounded together was all the shelter one needed. I liked the simplicity, and I laid there thinking how nice it was to live a simple life. I didn't have a watch, there was no need to know what time it was, and I didn't have to worry about being interrupted. I could just sleep, wake up whenever I wanted. No schedule to adhere to, no phones to annoy me, no television to pollute my head, no traffic to worry me, no newspaper to depress me. Just a simple roof over my head, the smell of the sea, the feel of a cool sea breeze through the open doorway, the songs of the birds circling endlessly above, and the roar of the surf to lull me to sleep.

When I awoke the sounds were the same, but the quality of light was different; early dusk. Also, I noticed that the wind was a bit stronger. It had been constant all day long, but it had gained in strength.

I went outside. The sun was nearing the horizon, indicating I had slept a few hours. The sun was obscured by clouds to the west, but there were darker ones to the north, the direction the wind was coming form. It looked like we would get a storm before too long.

The three others – Max, Franno and the Indonesian captain – were in the newer building talking and invited me to join them. It was a very small house but it looked very cozy. I estimated the house to be eight feet by twelve feet; a 96 square-foot house!

Max was sitting on a bed against the south wall, the Indonesian captain was sitting on a bed along the west wall, and Franno was sitting at a very small table along the north wall with a two-way radio on it. I sat in the doorway, in the center of all three of them. There were "windows" (no glass) in each of the walls with a shutter that swung out on hinges attached to the top of the window. They were all propped open halfway. There were shelves on the walls with a radio/cassette player and tapes (which Max was making the cabinet for) some books, cigarette packages, carved wooden figures, and other odds and ends. There were boxes, buckets and sacks under the beds. Spear guns were propped up in one corner, and nets hung in another corner. Hung on the south wall was a small ship's wheel. On it was painted "Max and Franno 1993."

Max saw me looking at the wheel. "That was our first," he said.

"What's it from?" I asked.

Helen's Reef was closer to Indonesia than it was to the main archipelago of Palau, and Indonesian fishing boats would occasionally try to illegally fish the reef waters. Max and Franno were there to protect the reef from these poachers. As policeman and radio operator they stayed on the island for three months at a time, and then another crew of two took over. They would be returning to Koror by ship in five days.

"We can see much of the reef from the island," Max was explaining to me. "We have binoculars. But we also patrol the reef on our speed boat. We could see a boat through our binoculars on the far end. They were trying to hide from us.

"We took our boat there. They didn't try to run because our boat is much faster than theirs. We went up alongside their boat to see who they were. They were from Indonesia fishing illegally. I boarded their boat. I had my gun with me, just in case." I never did see Max's gun, but he was proud he had one, and he was proud of his shooting ability.

He said they brought the illegal fishing boat back next to the island, secured it and radioed Koror. A ship was sent from Koror. The fishermen were taken back to Koror and incarcerated until they could be sent back to Indonesia.

"I got the wheel from that boat," Max said proudly. "I painted our names and the date on it."

"What happened to the fishing boat?" I asked.

"We burned it just outside the reef."

"I see," I replied.

As we sat and talked the wind got quite strong, the clouds appeared ominous and it began to rain. It looked as if we were to be hit with quite a storm. The three others were unconcerned, except for lowering the shutters to a crack, enough to keep out the rain but allow in some airflow. I knew enough to trust an islander's knowledge of weather, and so I, too, remained unconcerned.

Twenty minutes later the rain and wind had stopped and the ominous look of the clouds was gone.

"Why don't you go for a walk?" Max suggested. That seemed like a very good idea. "Dinner will be ready when you get back."

I took a slow walk around the small island. It was right about sunset time, and although there were too many clouds to make a colorful sunset, it was still a peaceful one. In the fading light I visited the birds at the west end and got close to some eggs, but didn't touch any. Terns nest on the ground and rarely lay more than a single egg at a time. I watched the movement of the thousands of birds in flight above, searched for interesting shells on the beach, inspected for signs of turtles, and scanned the beautiful horizon. There was still a little bit of light in the west when I returned. Dinner wasn't quite ready, but one of the captain's crewmen – the only one on the island from the fishing boat, acting as a cook – was busy making dinner. While we waited the cook brought me some tea, which tasted great.

"It's your birthday tomorrow," Max said as he pulled out a fifth of vodka. "So we celebrate!" He, Franno and the captain had big smiles on their faces.

"Do you like lemonade?" Franno asked.

"Yes."

"We made this from fresh Palauan lemons, water and sugar. I hope you like it. We'll drink it with the vodka." Franno poured everyone a glass and Max added vodka to each.

They all lifted their glasses and Max said, "To your happy birthday!" Before we could toast, though, the captain said something in Indonesian. Franno translated,

"He said he also wishes you a happy birthday and a good trip to Australia." I thanked him, and Franno and Max, and we drank.

We sat there drinking and talking as it became dark and we waited for dinner to be served. I did my best to talk to Franno and Max in Palauan, but occasionally had to revert to English. They were vary patient with me. I wasn't good in my Palauan, despite my six years in the country, but I was proud to speak it when someone was patient with me, and I wasn't sure when, or if, I would have the opportunity again.

The meal was simple, but very good: fresh fish soup and rice. They also opened some canned tuna and canned corned beef, but I was content with the fish – it was very well prepared and tasted fantastic. It seemed like they wanted to offer me more variety, but I was flattered that they had made me the guest of honor, and the food was more fresh than any restaurant could ever have hoped for. It was an easy and comfortable evening.

After dinner we moved to the little house and made ourselves comfortable, and lit some lamps. Franno talked on the radio to people from his and Max's home island, Tobi, then he put on some music while we all chatted. The Indonesian captain had brought some homemade whiskey which he called "redrum" because it was red and tasted like rum. Very clever. No connection, however, to the book The Shinning by Steven King. Out of respect I offered to try some, even though I thought my throat may not survive the experience. I was surprised, however, at how good it tasted, and it was smooth. The captain said that it was made from some variety of flower in Indonesia. It was good, and I enjoyed the company; I found myself very relaxed by the whiskey. I was still very tired from the trip and my lids were heavy, so I said that I would be turning in. Max insisted that I sleep in his bed. I did the Palauan thing and declined, but he offered again, which was my cue to gladly accept; it would be so good to sleep in a bed, even if it was just a foam mat on a plywood frame. I was asleep almost immediately. I woke up sometime later and the other three were still awake drinking at the table outside the house. I turned over and went back to sleep.

It was a wonderful feeling to wake up on my birthday on Helen's Island. I had had a very good sleep and I felt rejuvenated. The sun was already up but still very low in the horizon. I went for a walk around the island. The terns were making their perpetual patterns in the sky above which was accompanied by their calls; their presence was becoming familiar and comforting.

I found a number of interesting shells, and selected one small one to travel with me to Australia. There were more signs of turtles, which Max informed me later was where a turtle had laid eggs the night before. Sea turtles lay upwards of 200 eggs at a time, and are sometimes served at Palauan feasts. I also saw bits of an old turtle shell and interesting pieces of driftwood on the beach.

It was a beautiful day, and it was nice to take a solitary walk with just the sounds of the birds and the surf. I felt so peaceful at Helen's Reef, and I really felt comfortable with Max and Franno. I thought how wonderful it would be to stay at a place like Helen's Reef for a month or two or three, and just wind down, be with the wind, waves, water, birds, wind, clouds, sky, weather, my thoughts, my journal, and about a hundred books. What a luxury to have the time to put life in a new perspective. What an appealing thought this was. And it stuck in my head.

In my conversations with Max and Franno I learned that a ship would be coming in five days then returning to Koror. I actually began to consider staying on Helen's Island until that ship came – five wonderfully quiet days – and then return to Koror. Why not? It would give me five days on Helen's Island and I wouldn't have to leave Palau after all. I could resume my teaching job in Koror, I was sure, or I could even return to Helen's Island and get that new perspective on life.

These thoughts were very tempting.

I didn't need to return to the *Suena* until 3: 00 in the afternoon, so I still has some time to consider things. It was still early and the sun was still low but already it was getting intense. I headed back to the "Max and Franno Estates."

The others were up by this time and the captain's cook was preparing breakfast. The hot water was already done, so there was instant coffee. It really was satisfying.

Max, Franno and the captain all remembered to wish me a happy birthday. It was a happy birthday, and I let them know I was very pleased to be on Helen's Island, and I was glad I had their company on this special day.

Soon breakfast was done; fresh scrambled tern eggs, rice, and canned corned beef. It doesn't seem like the type of breakfast one would relish, but it seemed like a feast to me, especially since they treated me with such comfort and respect.

When we had finished breakfast and I was on my second cup of coffee I said, "I like it here so much!"

Both Franno and Max smiled with pride.

"You should come to Tobi," Franno said.

"I would love to."

"You know Mike?" asked Max.

"Yes," I replied. I remembered Mike as the man at the State Office back on Koror.

He was an American Peace Corps who had married a woman from Tobi.

"He stayed here for two months last year," Max said, then added, "You could do the same."

"Sounds great! I would love it."

"Come back. We'll teach you how to really fish!"

"Maybe I won't leave," I suggested.

"Stay in Palau," he affirmed.

"Maybe I should just wait here for the ship back to Koror and go on that. Then maybe I could come back to Helen's someday and stay for a longer time."

"Sure," Max said. "That would be no problem, and you could come here any time. You could even come and stay on Tobi."

That's what I wanted to hear. But was I reasonable even thinking about it? It was such an appealing idea. But was I crazy?

I spent the next few hours talking with Max and Franno about whatever came into our heads, exploring more of the small island with Max, admiring the beauty of Helen's, writing in my journal, and doing a lot of thinking. Then I took a nap. I felt I needed to make a decision. I was beginning to get anxious because the time to leave was drawing nearer.

It was nearing lunch and I was getting hungry. I was watching as seven fishermen from the Indonesian boat brought in huge rice bags filled with sea cucumbers and dumped them near the work shed. The captain began to explain to me the different varieties of sea cucumber, where they are found, how much each would sell for, where the good markets are, how they are smoked and cooked, et cetera. Franno and Max translated. The seven Indonesian fishermen, the few allowed from the boat to the island to work, began to build fires to smoke the catch. Some of the men would stay to finish preparing the catch, while the others would return to the fishing boat via the speedboat.

Max said, "Before we eat lunch let's go see the fishing boat."

"I would like that," I said.

A few minutes later I was getting into the speedboat with Max, the captain (who was operating the speedboat), and five of the fishermen.

It felt good to be in a speedboat again. The speed. The wind on my face. The changing horizon. The movement and bounce of the boat. And, believe it or not, the noise. There is something about riding in a speedboat that fills me with a sort of euphoria. The captain drove the boat very fast and liked to make sharp turns, which added to the thrill. The fishing boat was only about a half of a mile from the little island, so we were soon there.

We drew up alongside the fishing boat, tied up and we got on. I was amazed. It was no longer than the *Suena* and about as wide (but more square). There was a strong smell of fish, seawater and diesel fuel. There was a small open cabin that covered the back third of the boat. There were more large rice bags of sea cucumbers in the middle of the boat, along with diving tanks. I saw regulators, masks, gloves and other diving equipment hanging in all available places. On lines back by the cabin were hanging worn clothes. The planks were slippery and the boat was cluttered. I almost lost my footing, or tripped over things, numerous times in the five or ten minutes I was on the fishing boat. It felt cramped and crowded. I could hardly believe that fourteen people, plus the captain, lived on the boat. I could also hardly believe that they had all traveled a couple hundred miles across open ocean on that rickety jumble of wood I was standing on. It didn't seem like it could stand much of a sea. What would happen if they hit a storm? Or had engine problems? I guess those were the chances they took. That's how they lived – on the edge. Occasionally, fishing boats would drift to Koror, usually from the Philippines. One particular boat had been adrift twenty-one days before landing at Koror. Five fishermen had been on it. It was not that large, and in fact it was more like a canoe – five feet wide and thirty feet long, with outriggers. No shelter. When I saw the boat (a friend of mine was taking care of it while it was in Palau) I was amazed what people must endure to make a living to survive.

I could hardly imagine the life that the Indonesian fishermen I saw at Helen's Reef must have lived. They couldn't have made that much money, and I got the impression that they were worked quite hard by the captain. Their meals were meager rice and what fish they could catch. Also, they were stuck on the boat – the captain rarely let them go to the island, and only in small groups. I was palpably reminded how we Americans really have no concept of what it is like to live in a third world country, what it would be like to spend all our waking hours working for our next meal, with only dreams of what it would be like to have leisure time, a car, a DVD, a stereo, a house, a bridge club, and other luxuries we don't even recognize. Even indoor plumbing, a warm shower every day, or clean drinking water. I've been to the Philippines and have seen people living in "houses" of less quality than what most Americans would put their lawnmowers in. I imagined these guys had similar houses back in Indonesia.

I tried to keep my mouth from falling open as I looked around. I could see that most of the guys on the boat were staring at me; many of them, I imagined, had never before seen an American, except maybe in pictures. I wondered what they were thinking. Were they wishing they could trade places with me? Probably so, but I couldn't blame them. I'd want to change places too.

After a simple lunch back at Helen's Island – more rice and canned corned beef – the time to go back to the *Suena* was drawing near. Instead of the beach I took a short walk through the "bush." There was a small chapel less than 50 yards beyond the water tank hidden in the vegetation. It was quite dilapidated and looked as if no one had been in it for years. I carefully opened the front door, made of tin hung from one hinge, which made a grinding squeak. The seating capacity was probably ten on the bamboo benches before a simple wooden altar. There were no windows, but the crumbling wood allowed in considerable light. There was a vase in the corner behind the altar with the dried stems of some long dead decoration. A broken rosary hung on a nail next to one of the benches. I thought this might be a good place to sit and think. But soon after sitting the chapel just gave me the creeps. I stayed a few minutes trying to let the feeling dissipate, but it didn't. It was an interesting chapel and it reminded me of the ubiquitous presence of human beliefs. But I didn't feel comfortable there, so I left.

As I continued my walk I knew that, as much as I wanted to, I couldn't stay on Helen's Island with Franno and Max to wait five days for the ship. I knew I could get a job in Koror, and I knew I could probably even return to Helen's if I wanted to. But I also knew that I had to finish the dream, I had to complete what I had started – I had to sail to Darwin. Otherwise I would forever be wondering what it would have been like, and I didn't want the ever living questions in my mind. I still had some more adventure to experience in sailing, and I still wanted to see Australia. And also, Rick and Phyllis had wanted an extra crew member for assistance in sailing this long trip; I couldn't, with good a conscious, renege on my word.

So I resolved to look ahead with a positive attitude, and hope that one day I would again get the opportunity to set foot on Helen's Island.

Rick and Phyllis had moved the *Suena* closer to the channel entrance, which was quite a distance from the island, so the captain with Franno and Max drove me in the speedboat to the *Suena*. They decided to do some fishing while they were out in the speedboat, so they loaded their spear guns, masks and other fishing gear into the boat. Soon we were racing over different shades of blue and green water toward the shipwreck on the western reef.

There were no seats in the boat, so I was sitting on the edge holding on as best I could, although there wasn't much to hold on to. Franno was sitting on the back and the captain was piloting the boat in his wild ways. Max was standing at the front, holding on to a rope for balance. It didn't take long to realize that Max was navigating and the captain was following his cues. Max would point and the captain would steer, quite abruptly, in the direction Max indicated. I didn't know where Max was going. I knew where the *Suena* was; I could see the mast in the distance if I squinted just right, but we weren't heading in that direction. At first I thought we were heading to the shipwreck, maybe to get more wood so Max or Franno could build another cabinet, but that wasn't the case. Then I saw we were following something in the water. I saw an occasional dark shape in the water darting this way or that. Then I knew what they were. Turtles! Max was chasing turtles. Large ones. Two and a half to three feet long... or more.

Then I could see that Max's movements became more tense; we were getting close. Then suddenly Max was gone. He had jumped into the water. The captain let up on the throttle and we circled back to Max, bobbing in the water.

"Too small," he said as he climbed back into the boat.

His left arm was bleeding, but he didn't seem to notice. He stood back in front and had barely grabbed the rope when the captain had the engine gunned to full throttle. Within two minutes we were hot on the trail of another turtle. The same scenario followed and suddenly Max was overboard again. However, this time when we circled around he was struggling with a giant turtle. The captain pulled the boat up right next to Max and with amazing strength he lifted the turtle up to the boat. Franno helped Max get the turtle in. Max casually climbed back in. It was definitely a large turtle, at least three feet. No one made any comments and we were off again. This time we headed in the direction of the *Suena*; apparently one turtle was enough.

Turtles are one of the oldest living organisms to have inhabited this Earth; they've been around about 200 million years. Now many species, including this one, the greenback, are in danger of extinction. I personally have fought internally with the issue, living in a culture where turtles are eaten. Palauans still eat turtles, but they don't hunt the turtles for commercial or economic purposes, just an occasional feast or custom. Should these infrequent practices, which are environmentally sound on a local scale, be prohibited because of the avarice of other cultures? I hate to see the turtles in danger of extinction, but I also hate to see the Palauans lose out on their culture. Can both turtles and culture be preserved? It's an unfortunate dilemma.

Rick and Phyllis were in the dingy about 50 yards from the sailboat, and I could see they also had their fishing gear and snorkels. The captain killed the engine and we greeted the dingy. Small anchors were thrown, and everyone entered the water, snorkeling or spear fishing. I was one of the snorkelers.

I'd done a bit of snorkeling in the six years in the islands, but I had never experienced anything like Helen's Reef. The water we were in was only about 6 to 8 feet deep, plenty of light, clear, abundant with fish and life. The variety of fish and sea-life was amazing: sea anemone oscillating in the tide, clams of all different sizes covered with amazing electric colors, coral from sharp spiny varieties to ball-like and fan-like varieties, and hundreds of varieties of small many colored and patterned fish.

I leisurely swam with my snorkel enjoying the beauty, occasionally diving to the bottom to look at something closer. I saw a giant clam 3 to 4 feet long, which I dove down to inspect closer. It was so huge and colorful, beautiful and awesome. It was hard to believe it was real.

I continued on and came to a drop off. The reef slanted down at an incredibly steep angle, almost 90°. Looking down, the water was a deep marine blue, fading into black just a bit further on. The coral was larger and more impressive, and deeper down I could see larger fish also. I dove down a few times, but didn't get more than 20 or 25 feet. The water was noticeably colder there.

Heading back to the boat I saw Franno trying to get my attention. We surfaced and he asked, "Did you see that clam over there?"

It was the one I had been looking at earlier. "Yes!"

"Pretty, isn't it."

"Very!" I agreed.

He put his snorkel back in his mouth and was gone.

I returned to the boat and climbed in for a rest while the others continued to swim and fish. The turtle was still there on its back, gasping for breath, occasionally flapping its feet in a futile attempt to change its situation. Its gasping breaths sounded eerily like a human's. There was also a pile of fish flopping in the bottom of the boat. I sat there for a few minutes catching my breath, enjoying the late afternoon sun.

I felt a sadness of knowing I would be leaving on the morrow.

Then Franno's head popped up out of the water. He grabbed the side of the boat and flung in a large piece of flesh.

"I got it," he said proudly.

"Oh," I said, not quite knowing what he got.

"That giant clam," he said, seeming to read my mind. He smiled and disappeared in the water again. Max and the captain also popped up for just a few seconds each to throw in a few more fish. I put my mask and snorkel on and entered the water again. Sure enough, the giant clam I had seen earlier was now just a huge empty shell. Franno later told me that they rarely hunted turtles or the giant clams, but since they would be returning to Koror and family in five days (after so many months away) they wanted to have smoked food to bring back to relatives.

Later, back on the *Suena*, Phyllis was cooking dinner although it was my turn, she volunteered to do it since it was my birthday – Rick was below reading or something, and I was above deck brooding. Helen's Reef was such a beautiful place, and I had had such a good time with Max and Franno and the captain. But the next morning we would be leaving. I hated to leave, Helen's in particular and Palau in general. I looked around and was filled with awe and happiness at experiencing Helen's Reef, but it was mixed with a pain of knowing I may never see it again.

After dinner and dishes (which I also didn't have to do) Phyllis and Rick wished me a happy birthday and gave me a gift: a card, a very nice seashell, and a bottle of wine. We had some of the wine while we watched the sunset. I was quiet, I didn't have much to say. It was a beautiful sunset, as if to say, "Take one last look." I stayed above deck after sunset gazing at the stars, thinking and praying about things. About Palau, what I had experienced there, how it had become a part of me. Wondering if, when, and how I'd return. Wondering what life had in store for me once I returned to the states. Thinking about home, wanting to get there soon and see my family. Wondering about the rest of the voyage, how long would it be, worried about storms.

I went below deck, wrote in my journal for awhile, read a little, then went to bed early.

Chapter 4

Through the Doldrums

The morning sky reflected my mood: it was a steely grey, populated with clouds, the south dark. Even the water was ominously dreary. A lone shark's fin cut the glassy water.

As we left the ring of Helen's Reef I felt an almost physical pain, like leaving the safety of a mother's arms, leaving, the final time, my home of six years. I saw the lone tall palm of Helen's Island on the horizon recede as we sailed south. I said my last good-by in my heart, then turned around to face our destination; I wouldn't let my self look back. Even the bunch of bananas my Palauan friend had given me was staying on Helen's Island with Max and Franno. I felt very lonely and I wanted to get home to my family as soon as possible, yet we had quite a way to travel first.

It was about 10: 00 am when we left the ring of Helen's Reef; we woke up after sunrise, had a regular breakfast, and prepared the boat for our next leg. There was time for a few more hours of sleep, but I knew I wouldn't have been able to sleep that morning. When I got above deck the skies looked ominous to me; stormier than they had looked since we left Koror. One of my concerns on the trip was hitting storms. The thought of being in a small boat during a storm at sea frightened me, being tossed around in the middle of a raging sea, with no sailing experience, away from family and friends. It looked to me like that day may have arrived. I tried not to worry, knowing that the *Suena* was very seaworthy and capable of enduring storms. And besides, I told myself, Rick knew the *Suena* and had extensive experience with sailing. *He'll know how to handle any situation we will get in.* Rick listened to the weather reports twice daily, and he knew the weather patterns. He wasn't worried, so why should I? But I was. I couldn't help it. So instead of trying to rest, I stayed on deck and just watched.

There was actually a chill filling the air. Straight ahead of us, filling the horizon, was a wall of very dark clouds. Even behind us the clouds seemed to be developing into an angry formation and closing in. Above, in the steely clouds, were dark wisps moving in swirls that were reminiscent of Steven Spielberg special effects. At that moment how I longed to be in the movie theater, where it was safe and warm, with a box of popcorn! I was reminded of the book The Hobbit by J.R.R. Tolkien and how Bilbo Baggins kept wishing he were back in his cozy home, smoking a pipe in front of a warm fire. I knew how he felt many times on this voyage and this was one of those times. But he also had an exciting adventure; an interesting life doesn't come from sitting at home in front of the fire.

At that moment I was quiet and my heart was heavy. Rick was animated and seemed to enjoy my mood. That irritated me, but I was glad he wasn't looking concerned about the weather.

Then it started to rain. Our visibility was reduced and it was grey all around. My anxiety increased, and with it Rick's spryness.

"Yes!" he cheered, "This is sailing! The weather, the wind, the rain!"

I preferred the sun.

For the next two hours things went smoothly despite the look of things. I went below deck to try to read and rest before my watch – and try to forget my fears about the weather. But I couldn't. I stayed below deck for a while, but ended up going back above deck before too long.

When my watch began things were the same – grey, wet and cold. We were sailing, but not exceptionally fast. The sky continued to look ominously stormy, but the weather wasn't acting stormy, just gentle, rhythmic swells and a little rain. I was able to relax a bit with the present conditions – we were "smooth sailing" – but one thing bothered me … the southern sky. It was still very dark, the clouds were large and mean looking, and we were heading into the middle of it. Of course I didn't voice my fears because I didn't want to admit I was frightened. So why was I?

We continued, painfully slow, toward the ominous south. The only landmarks were the large clouds in the distance. In a sea stretching into infinity in all horizons, sailing can seem extremely slow. The ominous clouds only seemed to stay at a distance. Eventually we did get closer and even seemed to enter the dark clouds, but they never lived up to their threatening appearance. They were just dark and scary, but they had no bite. My watch saw no change except that eventually the rain stopped.

On we went. The weather stayed somewhat dreary, although we saw little more rain, not as many dark clouds and the swells were gentle. The stars even came out at night; the nights were still the best!

One night while I was on watch there was a huge bank of clouds ahead, the only clouds in the sky. The wall of clouds was massive and stretched from the right horizon to the left horizon. It towered high in the sky, was well defined, and the flat bottom was very dark. We were heading right for it, or, rather, right under it.

I could see torrents of dark rain falling from different sections of this huge bank of clouds, although straight ahead was clear. It looked like more special effects from some modern movie, but it was real, which made it so much more spectacular… and frightening.

I worried about it. I didn't want to hit rain. This was because Rick had warned Phyllis and I about squalls. He emphasized that they could be very dangerous. Rick said to call him if I ran in to a squall. I still wasn't quite sure what a squall was; I still hadn't experienced one so I still didn't know exactly when to call him. I would have called him just to look at the situation ahead, but I didn't want to wake him (especially with his grumbling). I hoped it wouldn't be too late when I realized we were in one. So we sailed on toward the impressive, and somewhat threatening, bank of clouds. I was experiencing two powerful emotions: Fear of the squalls, and awe at the spectacular scene before me. In the end, the beauty of nature was more intense, and I was able to relax enough to enjoy it. I can't describe how much more spectacular reality is than any Spielberg special effects.

As it turned out we sailed right under that bank of clouds, between two towers of heavy rain, the wind pressing us on. I was filled with rapture (and just a tinge of fear) the whole time.

On the third day from Helen's we saw the first islands of Indonesia. I was so excited to see them! After three days on the open ocean it was nice to see land again. But also, after leaving Helen's Reef I had a strong desire to get to home and family. I hadn't seen my family for a year, and after leaving Palau I wanted the comfort of home and family to mourn my loss. Seeing the islands of Indonesia meant that we were one step further along, another leg closer to home. We were now south of the equator (my first time!), and once we passed through the straight through Indonesia – right next to Sorong – we'd just about be close enough to see Australia. Well… not really, but it would feel like a major obstacle hurdled, and we would have a straight shot. Well… that's not completely true either. We would have a "dog leg" to do – two straight shots. But we would be closer to our goal!

Sailing was actually going very well, but my desire to get home was becoming very strong.

It was about 8:00 am when I went above deck. I could feel the excitement and couldn't sleep. Rick pointed out the islands in the distance to the west. It was good to see land again, even though we weren't going to set foot on land for quite some time yet.

As we continued south we spotted more and more islands. As we traveled I began to think more and more in terms of little goals to be achieved, rather than thinking ahead to the main goal of arriving in Darwin. At this point the next destination point in my mind was getting through the Indonesian straight, but even more immediate was getting to the straight "entrance." My hope was that we would at least enter the straight that day. But my hope would not be fulfilled.

The western mountains of Papa New Guinea – Irian Jaya – came into view. Rick told me that if you take the square root of the height in feet of a coastal land mass you could get the distance in miles at which you could first spot that land mass while out at sea. Pretty easy. He said the mountains we were seeing were approximately 5000 feet high, which would make us approximately 70 miles distant. It didn't seem that far. We were sailing very slow, as we had been for most of the last three days. We had also used the engine quite a bit, too, but this was to be expected since we were in the doldrums. The straight was further than we could see. It would be awhile.

The doldrums are an area near the equator – both north and south – where because the warm air near the equator rises, there is little wind along the surface for sailing. These latitudes were noticed by early mariners. Sometimes the winds would become so calm ships could be left drifting for days or even weeks. Avoided if possible, unless, like us, the ship had an engine. The oft used meaning today, of course, can mean inactivity, stagnation or even a depressed mood.

The day passed very slowly, and by the end of my watch it was obvious that we weren't going to get as far as I had hoped that day, so I tried to relax and enjoy the scenery. Rick had a nice pair of binoculars, which was a help.

By dinner time we began to see other boats; we had definitely arrived in Indonesian waters. It was a nice feeling to see other boats which meant there were still other people on the Earth. I would have loved to have gone ashore and explored for a time, met the people, experienced the culture and enjoyed Indonesia. Rick had mentioned before we left that there are still pirates in Indonesian waters, which I tried not to think about. But that was impossible. What a score an American yacht would be for Indonesian pirates! Another worry was that, to pass through this particular straight required permission from the Indonesian government, a visa or permit. We had neither. I didn't want to end up at the wrong end of a pirates gun – or scimitar – nor did I want to end up in an Indonesian prison because we didn't have the right piece of paper. I had seen the Midnight Express and I didn't want to be the Indonesian version. I hoped and prayed neither pirates nor prison would be our fate. I didn't think either would, but I couldn't help but worry a little. But I have to admit, these possibilities did make the journey more exciting.

By my night watch there was enough boat traffic to warrant full attention. Rick stayed up with me awhile explaining how to recognize if we were on a collision course with another vessel. There were a number of lights that could be seen from our position: villages, boats, lighthouses. Rick told me how to tell the difference, and how to use the lighthouses to navigate to our destination. The more immediate concern, however, was to avoid hitting other ships.

After explaining to me thoroughly what to look for Rick said, "If you think you are on a collision course, then let me know right away." He went below deck. To the east, beyond the immediate coast, I could see the glow of Sorong. Somehow the proximity of a city was comforting, although I had never heard of Sorong before. At a later time I looked up Sorong in a travel book and atlas. The atlas indicated the population was below 50,000. The travel book didn't say much more. The entry was short saying its economic base was petroleum and timber, and added if one must stay in this city of rough and tumble men playing pool between jobs, then there are two or three tolerable places to lodge, which it listed. It didn't recommend risking staying at any other places, nor did it list any attractions.

It wasn't long after Rick went below deck that a ship's light wasn't moving to the right or to the left from dead ahead. It was getting brighter. I gave it a bit more time – I didn't want to wake Rick for a false alarm – but it stayed dead ahead. I called Rick.

He came above deck and checked out the situation. After about a minute or two he said, "If you are on a collision course then you have to get out of the way. To do that just make a sharp turn, like this." He pushed the tiller hard to the port side turning the sailboat to the starboard. A minute later a ship twice our size motored past, bobbing our boat with its bow waves. I was amazed how close the other ship was – how the night diminishes perception! I was also surprised how calm Rick was about it. If I had waited another two minutes we might have been sinking along with another boat! "Don't be afraid to turn the ship," he said without the usual grumbling and went below deck.

I was losing out on sleep, for I woke again early and wasn't getting sleep between day and night watches, getting only a few hours of sleep in the mornings. But I was excited to be in Indonesia which helped me forget my tiredness. We were now close enough to get a good view of the land and see a lot of boats on the waters, and this was the day we would navigate the passage. It was nice to be so near land and see signs of people, and I especially liked the simple lifestyle of the non-Western world cultures. As I used the binoculars to view the landscape and watch the indigenous people fish the waters, I tried to imagine the daily lives of these people. Very different from my own, I was sure. They probably survived mostly on locally grown foods and the fish they caught in the straights, cooking it on kerosene stoves. They probably rose with the sun – or before – and retired with the sunset, maybe using kerosene lamps for a few hours of dim light in the evenings. Probably no telephones, no cars, no flush toilets. Maybe a radio, but not likely a television. Of course nearby Sorong was a city with all of these things, but even so, most people there probably lived simple lives with very few amenities. Maybe a few lived anything resembling a "middle class" lifestyle. Of course all this was all speculation, but probably not far off.

I enjoyed being in Indonesia, but I was also looking forward to getting through this straight, hoping that we would be through by the afternoon, beginning, then, on the next leg (the dog leg) of our journey.

Rick had been studying the map – one given to him by friends who had sailed the same straight years before, in the other direction. He was worried about this passage. Not only from what he said (I knew him well enough to read between the lines of what he said, to know he was more nervous than what he led on), but the quality of his voice and his body language were what really gave him away. He had said that he wanted both Phyllis and I up on deck for this passage to help, watch the depth gauge, watch for landmarks, man the tiller, leaving him free to consult maps and charts and do the navigating. I was more than happy to oblige. There was no way I could have stayed below deck for this passage – watching land and signs of people was too much of a luxury to miss, and I had to see what Indonesia was like – I was only a stone's throw away from a vastly foreign land.

It was a beautiful day, there was a light wind and we were under sail moving at a leisurely pace. We were in the straight, but it was still fairly wide, like a bay. There were quite a number of ships in the bay. There were a few larger ships – two or three times larger than the *Suena* – but most of them were small fishing boats, a common person's boat. They all had the same or similar designs: about ten or twelve feet long, very skinny with an outrigger, and a small sail. They looked so frail and unstable; I was surprised they could float and stay upright, but they did. One sailed past the *Suena*, about fifty feet away. I wanted to examine the boat with the binoculars, but I felt that would be rude, intrusive, so I just looked from the corner of my eye. Sailing in the boat were a man and a woman; I presumed they were husband and wife. The man had one hand on the tiller and the other hand on the sail sheet. The woman had a fishing line in her hand. Both had big smiles for me as they sailed past. As they moved away from us I got out the binoculars and surreptitiously watched them sail away. How nice, I thought, to have such a simple vessel to sail on the bay every day. However, I'm not sure I would want to get my food in that way – everyday, but it's probably better food than from a can or a frozen package.

As the straight got narrower and narrower Rick got more and more tense. We lowered the jib and staysail and used the motor. There were lighthouses to guide the way, but Rick would not use them. Part of this was because the keel of the *Suena* extended five feet down into the water, much more than the average boat, and this straight had, according to the maps and charts, some very shallow sections. Rick wasn't trusting the charts, so he was quite nervous. I remembered he didn't trust the map of Helen's Reef either.

The landscape was very beautiful so it was a spectacular passage. It would have been more fun and leisurely if Rick wasn't so on edge. He was standing on the prow with a compass and a folded up chart. Phyllis was at the tiller steering to Rick's instructions. I would read the depth finder when Rick asked for a reading, but otherwise I had nothing to do. Unfortunately, I had to listen to Rick and Phyllis spat, which had become quite frequent. Mostly Rick was criticizing Phyllis concerning her steering, but he could find anything to criticize her about. I'm no expert, but it seemed like the conflicts went much deeper than the petty things they argued about. It was, after all, their last sailing trip together, and there was always the question of why they had decided to part ways. I did my best to ignore their own personal struggles and enjoy the beautiful panorama around me. And it was beautiful!

Indonesia was much like Palau in many ways: colors of the waters, the thick green of foliage, the terrain. Yet it was also different. I saw birds I hadn't seen in Palau, and heard unfamiliar sounds. I also noticed there were different varieties of trees, some very tall and massive, others of strange shapes. But mostly it just felt different.

We spent the day moving through the straight at a snail's pace – Rick's extreme caution and the currents against us were the main cause. Rick had taught me enough about how one could navigate by lighthouses that I could see the course they delineated through the straight. But Rick wasn't following this simple path.

"Don't the lighthouses indicate to go in this direction?" I asked Rick as meekly as possible, pointing out a different path than we were moving in.

"Yes," he conceded, "but they didn't have sailboats in mind when they set up those lighthouses."

"You mean," I asked, "the route marked by the lighthouses wouldn't be more than five feet deep?"

"Five feet wouldn't be enough for the *Suena*," he replied somewhat irritated and not really answering my question.

"Well, yeah," I corrected myself, "but wouldn't a major passage like this be at least ten feet? Wouldn't that be enough for us to travel through?"

"You have to remember," he continued with the same irritation, "that we also have to consider the tides, and we have very low tides today. Plus I don't trust these charts; these Indonesian charts aren't made very accurate, one rock marked five feet off – or not marked at all – would be disaster for us. We don't want to get stuck in Indonesia with a broken down boat."

I really couldn't argue with him; I wasn't the captain, therefore I wasn't making the decisions, and he did have a point. Plus I didn't have the same experience and time-proven judgment. Rick did. But it also didn't stand to reason – for me, at least – that if the charts were not trustworthy for the path outlined by the lighthouses, then the charts wouldn't be trustworthy for any other circuitous route either. It was frustrating to see boats three to five times larger than the *Suena* ripping through the passage with no problems. It was hard for me to believe that there wasn't enough water in the passage for the *Suena* to also make the same straight line safely through the passage marked by the lighthouses. Wouldn't that be the best possible route? But Rick trusted only his way – which seemed to take us through the most out of the way route possible – and so we were going slow ... painfully slow.

My hope of emerging through the south end of the straight by afternoon or early evening was dying fast. Scenery was changing slowly, and there was always more to go – the light at the end of the tunnel wasn't shining through. At least the unfamiliar and beautiful sights helped to keep me distracted.

Afternoon came and there was still more to go. I still had hope, though. I looked at the charts myself, and saw that the last section of the straight should be easy, no major dangers, it was deep, and well marked with lighthouses. The last passage could appear at anytime, and we could get out the last section, before nightfall. The hope was increased with the knowledge that the currents would be favorable for us – very favorable – beginning at about 6: 00 pm. But Rick began to talk about anchoring for the night. I didn't want to be so pretentious as to tell Rick how to captain his ship, but I did drop a few hints.

"The tides will be high at 6:00 pm, then the currents will change direction, flowing out the last section of the channel, right?"

"Yes," Rick agreed, "but the sun will be setting at that time, too, and I don't want to try the passage in bad light."

"The last section of the channel is deep, isn't it? And aren't there lighthouses clearly marking that last section?"

"There are," Rick agreed, but with rising irritation, "but it's a narrow channel, and the lighthouses may not be set in accurate places."

I still didn't agree with him, but I knew not to press the issue any further.

It was getting later and our progress was minimal. Rick began picking out a place on the map where we would anchor. My hopes were dying. I tried not to focus on the goal of getting out, but to take it as it came, enjoy the moment, knowing that morning wasn't far. But it was difficult. The trip was already nine days long, we were only about halfway, and I had mentally planned on a 10-day to two week trip. Obviously we weren't going to make that goal. But the worst part of it was my growing desire to just be at home, and stopping for the night was going to mean one more day from home. In a way I was between homes; I wasn't in Palau and I wasn't in Colorado. I was finding that it wasn't easy being in between.

But also, there was the fact that we were in the straight illegally; anchoring didn't seem like a good idea, especially so near a main line of ship traffic. Rick was aware of this, but he still wanted to anchor.

We anchored at the place Rick had chosen from the charts, just out of the path of ship traffic; a weak attempt to be incognito. I still thought we could have done it, completed the straight before nightfall. The sun was low in the horizon, but it was still visible, and I knew once it set we would still have enough light left for much of the channel. The currents were now in our favor and would be strong, the tide was high, and the lighthouses were clearly visible. I felt we could have done it. It was angering and frustrating, but I felt I had no recourse.

Our anchor point was about 100 yards off the shore. No villages or signs of human habitation were visible, and the map showed no villages nearby. All we could see were a few small islands, the ship channel only 50 yards to the west (with an occasional boat passing by), and Irian Jaya to the east. It was total jungle. I had never seen jungle so thick or trees so large, nor I had I heard such jungle sounds. This definitely was not Palau anymore. The stereotypical image of jungle is from the movies, especially Tarzan. In many ways this was similar, but it was so… real. Even if some of the sights are the same as in the movies, being there is so different. No explanation is possible to explain the actual experience.

I'm not sure what all the sounds I heard were, but imagined some of the sounds to be monkeys, but most of the sounds had to be birds. The birds were incredible. Rick had the binoculars and was searching the shore line jungle. He was letting out sounds of amazement.

The light was fading fast, so when it was my turn with the binoculars I couldn't make out details very well, but it was still an incredible sight. The number and colors of the birds! One very large tree was filled with hundreds of white cockatoos! It was amazing.

It was a very strange feeling being there. I had to keep telling myself it was real, that I really was in Indonesia. I had never dreamed that I would be in such an "exotic" place. It was exciting being were I was, but there were also some real concerns. Hearing all those sounds that were so foreign to my ears I couldn't help but to imagine head-hunters and painted bodies sniffing out the *Suena*, swimming the hundred yards of water and finding a good meal sleeping in this strange looking boat. I knew it was such a ridiculous thought, but it was there.

A more realistic thought also filled my head: Local peoples seeing an American boat in the water and imagining a lot of neat American things they would like to have. I could imagine us being robbed in the middle of the night. Pirates are very real in Indonesia, and I was sure people noticed the American yacht sailing through the straight – we were the only Western-looking sailboat I saw, and we traveled slowly enough for everyone to get a good look. Word travels fast, so I knew we were no secret. If something happened to us, who would know? Especially since we were illegal and not even supposed to be there.

Barring these wild improbable imaginings, we were still close to the channel and could be easily seen; I worried that an official boat of some kind would pass by and notice us, decide to check for our papers. Spending time in an Indonesian prison wasn't a good option either.

To top it all off I heard Phyllis say to Rick, "What about mosquitoes?"

He looked at her with a questioning look.

"Malaria," she said.

"Oh," he replied, "I didn't think about that."

Me either.

Rick got out the mosquito nets and we closed all openings, or covered them with mosquito nets. After a simple dinner we all went to bed early.

When I awoke the sun hadn't crested the horizon yet, but the pre-dawn light was enough to read by if I sat on the steps leading up to the deck. I didn't go outside because of the mosquito nets.

I hadn't been reading long when Rick saw me – he was awake too – and said, "It's Okay to go outside; the mosquitoes aren't out this early in the morning." Somehow that didn't strike me as valid. It seemed to me mosquitoes liked the coolness of the evening as well as the morning. What's the difference? But I trusted Rick and went outside. It wasn't more than two minutes before I was slapping mosquitoes on my legs and arms. Oh, what the hell, I thought, if I get malaria it will just add to the story of this adventure. And besides, we had to get an early start: High tide would be between 6: 00 and 7: 00 am, then the tides would reverse and we would then have unfavorable currents, which we wanted to avoid.

Soon Rick and Phyllis were up and we were getting the *Suena* ready for another leg of the journey. When we checked everything and all was secure for another open ocean crossing, we started the engine (for navigating the last channel of the straight) and raised the anchor. Phyllis operated the tiller and headed us through the last section of the straight.

"Can you help me with this?" Rick asked me.

"Sure," I said. "What do you want me to do?"

He came to the prow of the boat where I had just raised the anchor.

"We're going to stow the anchor; it will be better to have that weight closer to the center of gravity, than at this end of the boat where it can make the rocking worse in the open seas."

"Makes sense," I replied. "Why didn't we do it for the last open ocean crossing?"

"Well," he began, "it probably would have been a good idea, but his next crossing, especially the last section from New Guinea to Australia, could very well be rough. I want to take every precaution."

"You can feel the difference?" I asked.

He paused a moment and answered, "After a lot of sailing experience, Yes, I can feel a bit smoother ride. And," he added, "it's safer without that extra torque arm rocking the boat."

We used the halyard line to help lift the anchor and bring it aft, the whole time I was wondering what Rick meant when he said the waters could very well be "rough." For some reason the idea of a storm was making me nervous, but I tried to think about the task at hand instead.

The last section of the straight was like traveling on river about a quarter mile wide. The tide had changed so there was a current against us. It wasn't too bad yet, but would get worse. We were motoring so we didn't have to sail in the narrow straight, against the current, and there was very little wind. There was thick jungle on both sides. The trees were mesmerizing with their sheer size. There were occasional houses built of bamboo and thatch among the trees and reeds along the shore, with wooden pathways leading into the darkness of the jungle. We also crossed a few small villages. Only one or two small boats passed us in the other direction. It turned out to be a very leisurely morning, and I ended up enjoying myself. The scenery was enough to keep my mind occupied and distracted.

There was no navigating to do, just follow the passage – Rick was much calmer, which was nice. I used the binoculars to view the jungle, trees, houses and villages. I kept telling myself, "This is Indonesia!"

It was near my watch when we were exiting the straight at last. We were now beginning the last major leg (the dogleg) of our journey!

Chapter 5

Starting the Dog Leg

We had two options for this last major part of the journey: One, go basically straight south, which would be the most direct route, but would require careful navigation through the chain of the Seram Islands and later around Kepulauan Tanimbar. The other route was to skirt the southern coast of Inrian Jaya in a southeast direction, then turn to go south-southwest between Kepulauan Kai and Kepulauan Aru. This second route would require less between-island-navigation, but was a bit longer.

As far as I was concerned, I just wanted to get to Australia. We were on the tenth day of our ten-day trip, but we were only halfway to our destination. I was leaning toward the straight south path thinking a straight line is the shortest distance between two points, and thus the fastest route. But Rick, a more seasoned sailor than I, was also considering the predominant wind patterns for that time of the year. For that time of year the wind would be coming from the south or south east, which could mean we could be beating into the wind if we took route one, especially the very last part into Darwin through the Timor Sea. Rick thought if we skirted the Irian Jayan coast we might have wind from the front, but he was hoping it would be of less strength and less head on. Also, the last part of the second route would mean a better wind angle for us into Australia.

"If we go straight south," Rick said, "we might have to do a lot of tacking, which would make the going very slow." He chuckled and added, "You think we've been going slow up to now!" He showed me the route on the map, "But if we go this way," he traced the second route with his finger, "then the wind won't be so head on. We may have to tack some, but we might get by by close-hauling." He paused a moment then said, "I just hope the winds aren't really strong." He didn't say anything more.

I didn't respond right away either, but my mind was working.

Finally I asked, "Those could be strong winds?" I tried not to emphasize the word "strong."

"Some of those predominant winds just north of Australia can get pretty strong."

"That's good for sailing, right?" I asked doubtfully.

"Not if they're too strong. But we can always reef the mainsail and put up the small jib. We should be okay as long as we don't hit a storm."

I didn't ask any more questions.

By the time we left the straight through Indonesia, Rick had decided we would take the second route, the dog leg. I didn't look forward to the long distance we would have to travel, but I realized it was probably the best plan under the circumstances.

I didn't know it then, but we would pass near islands that Alfred Wallace Russell explored when he was forming his theory of evolution at the same time that Darwin was. I'm sure it would have provided me a little bit of comfort just knowing I was looking at the Kai Islands, and my mind could have been occupied thinking about what it would have been like for Mr. Wallace to have explored those islands over a hundred years before. Alfred Wallace Russell essentially drew the same conclusion as did Charles Darwin – over long periods of time species change to adapt to their environment. Russell and Darwin had even corresponded. With a little prompting by friends Darwin had published first. If he hadn't, we might have a term other than Darwinism… Russellism. Now that's a thought.

When it was my watch we were still in the delta area of the straight entering into the sea, and we were still using the engine since there wasn't enough wind for sailing. Unfortunately, the currents by this time were also quite strong against us. There was quite a bit of reef in the area so the waters were fairly shallow.

"These waters are confused," Phyllis commented. She was right. When we had been on the open ocean the swells were evenly spaced and moved in a smooth predictable way. Sometimes there were swells moving in two or three different directions, but they were easily distinguishable from each other. Closer to islands there were smaller wave patterns reflecting off of nearby islands, but again they were recognizable patterns. The waters in the delta had no patterns except they were rough and choppy, sharp and pointy, instead of smooth and predictable. With no wind, currents against us, and choppy waters, the *Suena* was moving at an agonizing one knot, sometimes less. This is slower than a slow walk, literally the speed of a crawl. I felt as if we would never get to sailing again. My watch seemed to go on and on and on, and the *Suena* seemed to make no progress at all. During my four hour watch we only made between four and six nautical miles of progress, which made the islands in the distance seem to remain in the same relative positions, giving the impression we were stationary.

I thought of this as our last major leg, but for sanity sake I had to divide this leg into two smaller legs: our skirting of Irian Jaya, and the crossing from Irian Jaya to Australia. Rick said it would take three to five days for the first part. In my mind I said, "Three days. We can do it in three days." I looked forward to the time we would turn the *Suena* south toward Australia.

After my watch I just wanted to sleep, escape from the slowness, but, unfortunately, sleep does not always easily come to me. I went below deck so I wouldn't have to see the same islands in the distance, not moving, hoping when I returned up top they would be at least in a slightly different position. I tried to read a book I had picked up in a store just before I left Koror, but even that book was going slow. I looked forward to the evening drink, but we were running out of alcohol, too. Things weren't looking good.

I had been doing fine, but as the journey looked to drag out I was beginning to get bummed. I loved the sailing we had done, but we had used the engine so much already by this point it was very discouraging. Instead of getting closer, Darwin seemed to get further away. The *Suena* was getting smaller. Rick's lack of encouragement and often scolding were irritating me. I wanted to get home. And the slow pace was getting old. I had a helpless feeling because there was nothing I could do about it. I couldn't make the engine go faster, I couldn't create wind, and I couldn't get off and take alternative transportation. I would fantasize about stopping at a port and flying the rest of the way, but I was hit with the reality that Darwin had the closest commercial airport!

So I just waited. Waiting might not have been so bad if I could have occupied myself in ways I knew how to relieve stress or energize a positive attitude. What I really wanted to do was go for a walk, play in the park, ride my bicycle, go for a drive, climb a tree. Nope. Not possible. Even reading, which was usually an uplifting experience for me, was getting me down – I had chosen a dud of a book and I couldn't get into it. It wasn't giving me the escape that I wanted. I wanted to be able to go somewhere. Not that I wasn't somewhere at that moment, and not that weren't moving, but … I was just bummed.

Talking to a friend would have been uplifting. I thought of Pilo. I remembered a time when she had asked if we could do one of our occasional lunches. She wanted to tell me something. It sounded important. We met at a park near the water called Long Island – obviously a take on the name of the island of the same name in New York. Very different, though. The Palauan Long Island was between Koror and Malakal, a small stepping stone between the larger islands. Very beautiful, as all the islands of

Palau were. A small park had been set up off the main road, a few picnic tables set up. A good place for swimming. It had become quite popular. A perfect place for lunch. Of course we had the usual: canned tuna, rice, kimchee, M&Ms and soda.

When we had finished our simple meal there was a lull in the conversation. She looked nervous, which was unusual when she was with me. I could see her hands trembling. What she had to say must have been important.

"Um…," she said, hesitating. I waited. She continued, "I wanted to tell you something." She paused again. It seemed hard for her.

I said, "Go ahead," to encourage her.

"We're good friends, right?"

"Yes, definitely."

"Well, as friends I feel I need to tell you how I feel." She stopped, thinking. She seemed to be stuck.

"Is it about me?" I asked, prompting.

"Yes," she said and smiled, but then looked nervous again. She seemed to be struggling for the words to say. Finally she continued, "I can't stop thinking about you. When I wake up in the morning you are the first thought in my head, and you are the last thing I think about before I go to sleep. When I go to prayer I can't get you out of my head."

She stopped. I waited. She didn't seem to know what to say next. It seemed like she wanted to say something, but just couldn't.

I said, "Are you trying to say you are attracted to me?"

She let out a nervous laugh and said, "Yes, I am attracted to you."

We both smiled. I said, "I've felt the same way about you. For a long time now. You are all I think about, too."

After a moment she said, "But…"

I knew what was coming next.

"But I have my vows."

I nodded.

"When I took my vows I meant them. And they are forever, so I intend to keep them."

"That's good," I said, trying to be understanding.

"I have to keep them."

"I know."

"This is very hard for me."

She meant telling me was hard, but she meant not pursuing her feelings was harder. For me too.

We talked some more. It was good to get our feelings out. It made things easier. But it was still very hard to be in love with someone who could never be available to me.

"But I still hope we can be friends." She seemed afraid I would say no.

"Friends forever," I said.

If anything, that made our friendship stronger and deeper. I longed to talk to her very much at that moment on the *Suena*.

Talking to Rick was out of the question, and although Phyllis was a nice person and I felt comfortable with her, she just wasn't the close friend I wanted to talk to. Listening to the radio would have been nice, even watching television. Not even that was available. All I could do was wait. Day and night.

Night! That was my salvation. I still had the night watch!

And even though the days were agonizing, the nights were still glorious. There was something about the night that filled me with awe, peace, joy and mystery. It never failed me, even if it was cloudy and I couldn't see the stars. So I held on to night as my savior; it was the thing that kept me sane throughout the trip, especially when I began to get stir-crazy. Somehow, at night the *Suena* became large, and I didn't feel cramped. The world came alive: sparkling stars (when visible, but even when not, I knew they were there), cool breezes, fresh smells, the feeling of the presence of life in the sea around me. My spirit soared.

I had by this time developed a routine for night watch. Phyllis would wake me, I would use the head and clean up, change into my above-deck-clothes, gather my five cassette tapes, get a drink of water and grab a handful of cookies before going up on deck. Up top Phyllis would give me bearings to keep the *Suena* on, and any other instructions I might need to know while on watch. When Phyllis went below deck I would check the course and other navigational information, look at the stars and constellations to get myself oriented as to our direction in relation to the sky, take note of the weather and waves, and if we were sailing I would check the sail trim and wind-vane steering apparatus. After about ten minutes of getting acquainted with the situation and surroundings, walking around the boat, I would stand in a comfortable position – usually facing forward with my arms resting on the cockpit canopy – and spend 15 to 30 minutes in meditation, checking occasionally, of course, our bearing and the horizon. It was during that half an hour or so that I really felt a connection with Spirit and the universe. It was that special time each day that gave me what I needed to make it through another day. During the day when I was feeling the lowest I would look forward to that time of meditation on my night watch. It kept me going.

After that special time I would move around the *Suena* to get a little "exercise." Moving my muscles felt good, and the feel of the oscillating boat was soothing. My movements and mind also perked up because I wasn't hooked into the safety lines and I knew one miss-step could very well be fatal. Although I never came close to stumbling, not being hooked into the safety lines added a challenge that I needed, even if it wasn't the smartest thing to do. Then I would sit and revel in the beauty of the night, thinking about whatever came to my mind, which was often Palau, Pilordes or home. Occasionally I would move around the sailboat just for the movement, and I would often check the bearings to keep on course, check the horizon for other ships, check the sails for trim, making needed adjustments. I felt proud that I had learned enough to feel comfortable – and be trusted – to keep the sailboat on course and sailing smooth.

I would wait until my watch was at least half over before I would allow myself the luxury of listening to a tape on my walkman. This made listening more sacred, more treasured. Plus, I had to conserve batteries. Also, in the second half of my watch I would allow myself the luxury of a second handful of cookies. Such small luxuries, but they became important to me, and the ritual of it – especially waiting – also made it more meaningful.

About a half an hour before I was to wake up Rick, I would put everything away and ready the boat for Rick's watch. Then I would spend the rest of the watch thinking and enjoying the predawn and begin to look forward to a good sleep – I slept best after my night watch.

The next few days I thought I would go crazy. We seemed to be going against currents most of the time, and when we did have wind it was usually against us. The wind was at such an angle that we could close-haul, but that wasn't getting us there very fast, especially against currents. (Close-hauling is when the wind is essentially from the front, but the sails are angled to still allow the boat to move forward, although slowly. There is a limit, however. You can close-haul when the wind is 30° to 45° off the dead-on front, not if the wind is straight on.) I would wake up in the morning and the landforms would be different, which was encouraging, but during my day watch they seemed to stay in the same positions, emphasizing our slowness. All I could do during my watch was sit (or stand) there and stare at the same, unchanging scenery. I couldn't go for a walk, and I couldn't move around much. We were using the engine quite a bit, forcing me to remain stationary, tiller in hand, the entire watch. Otherwise I could have at least moved around the boat for a change of position, or I could be free to read.

I tried to change my attitude, but it was so hard. I tried different things to cheer myself up. Usually reading helped me, but the book I was reading just wasn't doing it. I was tempted to put it down, but I was determined to finish it.

I also tried to listen to the walkman during the day, but when I listened to the five tapes I had they only depressed me more. I resolved to listen only at night – the only time I enjoyed music.

My daytimes were a "desert experience." I was surrounded by water that was full of life, but absent were those things that fed me in terms of my spiritual life, social life, and my daily routines. I had built up purpose in my life through my daily routines, or at least created an illusion that I was accomplishing something important. It was sort of a distraction from thinking about what my life really consisted of, who I really was, especially in the setting of the larger picture. I found that this "desert experience" was an opportunity to evaluate the ways I had found joy and meaning in my life away from my usual perceptions. Part of my "desert experience" was to embrace meaning apart from accomplishment, which is what the world tells us meaning comes from. I say I like to live simply, but this is part of the simple life – meaning apart form accomplishment, apart from material things, apart from experience. This experience really gave me time to think about my own meaning in life, and my connections to others and what they meant to me.

My thoughts went back to Palau. In addition to teaching, I also had the opportunity to visit other schools – high schools and the community college – to speak to young people about preparing for college and the transition to life away from the islands. One of my favorite trips was to the village of Ngaraard to the high school there, Bethania.

It was an all day affair, and a beautiful day for a trip to the big island. Ngaraard was about 30 miles, but by boat – the only way to get there – it would take at least two hours. That morning we pointed toward Babeldoab (the big island of Palau), the wind in my face, the sparkle of the blue water in my eyes, and the busy-ness of the "city" of Koror behind us, I could feel the pressures of my life lift and a lightness descend on my heart.

We skipped across the water at an incredible speed. With the wind, the boat bouncing on the water and the sound of the engine all made conversation an inconvenience, which was okay with me; I loved the scenery and the time to think. Flocks of birds were diving over schools of fish, there was an occasional speed boat in the distance going in a different direction, the green of Koror getting smaller behind us, and the banana and palm leaves soon became distinct ahead.

We headed northwest from Koror for the southwest tip of Babeldoab, then rounded the tip of the large island and headed north, up the west coast of Babeldoab. Looking down over the side of the boat I could see reef and sand basins race past only a few feet under the water. After about two hours of enchantment (and one stop on the way), the boat suddenly turned toward the mangrove and slowed down. In a nook in the coast was a small dock, which the boat driver steered toward, being careful not to hit any of the large coral growths hiding just beneath the waves, all of which he knew by memory. Without the wind of the racing boat to mask the heat, I could suddenly feel how intense the sun had become; I was glad I had put on a liberal amount of sunscreen before we left (although later I would realize that I had forgotten the tops of my feet – ouch!).

We had arrived at Ngaraard. We (I was traveling with two Public Health nurses and a social worker, Humie, from the Behavioral Health Division, who was working with me) loaded ourselves into a rusty, squeaky pickup. We drove along a well maintained dirt road through jungle, past taro patches and a few simple houses to the village on the east shore; it took us about ten minutes. The nurses got off at a house across from the elementary school, which seemed to be the center of the village. Humie and I remained in the back of the pickup and soon we passed under tall palm trees, through thick foliage, and over a small bridge emerging into a compound of buildings, mostly made from cinderblock and cement. A cement sign announced "Bethania High School."

The principal of Bethania – a Palauan woman in her late thirties – met us as we got out of the back of the pickup and introduced herself as Limasang. The pickup drove away as Limasang immediately began to usher Humie and I toward a large classroom where students were assembling – we were late.

The building was typical for Micronesia, constructed of cinder block, cement and rebar, a corrugated tin roof, many windows to circulate air, but no glass, no louvers and not even screen. The walls were painted white, yet stained from water and mold. Geckos on the walls and ceiling were chasing flies and mosquitoes, wasps' nests resided in the corners, a chalkboard at the front of the room desperately needed another coat of paint (chalkboards typically were wood painted with black paint).

Humie and I were led to benches where we sat while Limasang assembled some of the girls at the front of the room. Limasang said, "A song for our guests." The girls' sweet voices filled the room with a song about Jesus. When they finished they sang another. They were very good singers and I could tell that they enjoyed and believed what they sang. It was nice to see teenagers sing with such unconscious enthusiasm.

After the two songs the girls returned quietly to their seats and Limasang took the podium to address the student body. She introduced me as the "Doctor from the hospital." Although I was under the auspices of Behavior Health with Humie, I was far from being a doctor. But I didn't correct Limasang – I was too embarrassed, and then I also felt guilty. I approached the podium. As I arrived Limasang put a freshly made lei around my neck and a marmar on my head. The fragrance was strong and pleasant. The student body clapped, some giggled. Limasang took a seat near the rear door leaving me alone at the podium.

I looked toward 76 high school girls who were all wearing white blouses and green skirts, had black hair, dark skin and curious brown eyes all focused on me. I had given this talk to high schools in the islands before, but I was still nervous. A few teachers were standing at the sides, some looking discouraged that their class time was being usurped.

My talk was about fifteen or twenty minutes, mostly about being prepared for college and the related transitions. When I finished I asked if there were any questions. There was no response. It was an uncomfortable silence, a roomful of girls staring at me. I couldn't tell if they just wanted to have it done and get back to their own business, or if I had failed to speak on anything of interest to them.

I encouraged them not to be afraid, but also explained I would be available afterwards if anyone wished to speak to me or Humie. I saw a few girls whisper to each other. Then one raised a timid hand.

"Yes," I said acknowledging her.

"Doctor," she said, "does it cost anything?"

"No," I answered.

There were no more questions.

Walking away I couldn't help but feel that my presentation was a bomb, but at least, I told myself, the trip has been beautiful.

Limasang led us to a small bamboo gazebo with benches to relax on. It was a very comfortable place; cool with a light breeze, shady with only a few speckles of sunlight, sandy floor, the benches were surprisingly comfortable and the heat did not seem to penetrate the canopy of the breadfruit trees. The white sandy beach was only about fifty yards distant, the reef about a quarter mile out. The sound of the waves breaking on the reef was distant and hypnotizing. Humie and I had about two hours before our ride returned us to the dock to catch our boat. But two hours would pass quickly telling stories with Humie, playing cards, reading a book, enjoying the beauty and even napping. And although I had offered to be available for questions, after the non-response of the students I was sure there would not be any takers.

The students were on break and a number gathered under the shade of the trees not far from us, talking and laughing. Limasang excused herself to attend to the unending duties of a principal. A few minutes later a group of students joined Humie and I, fidgeting and shy. Finally one said, "We have some questions for you."

"Okay," I said,

They hesitated, looking at each other. Then one girl gathered the courage to say, "We wanted to talk privately."

"Oh," I replied a little surprised. "We can do that."

Then the girl who had spoken pointed to the girl next to her and said, "Her first."

They all giggled, but the girl who was pointed at didn't protest. For the next two hours I had one-on-one conversations with four different students. As there was not a private room to talk in we just walked closer to the water and sat on a large piece of driftwood in the white sand, at the edge of the shade of the large trees. The conversations were quiet and the sound didn't travel that far, especially with the roar of the reef nearby.

Very little of the conversations had anything to do with my presentation. One girl talked about her father, who wanted her to be a doctor. That was why he sent her from the islands of Yap to attend Bethania High School in Palau, to get a good education to get into a good university and eventually become a doctor. And although a good student, she didn't want to become a doctor. She was interested in becoming an actress. How could she reconcile this with her father's wishes?

The second girl talked of a good friend – also a student of Bethania – who started to spend more time with another student. The girl speaking to me was feeling jealous, and her friend was acting "weird" toward her.

The third talked also of a friend at Bethania who had been getting good grades but was now slacking off and becoming distant and quiet. She was worried her friend would get kicked out of school and have to leave Ngaraard and go back to her home village.

I felt all three of these students were looking for advice, and I felt comfortable enough to oblige them, at least with tidbits. Mostly my responses were to talk to someone they trusted, who was wiser: a teacher, the principal, a parent, an auntie or uncle. I also recommended speaking – as non-threatening as possible – to their friends or family about what was on her mind. Often talking directly to a friend solved the concern. I was careful to keep my advice safe, but yet give some direction.

Upon reflection I realized my advice was very Western, and although not necessarily wrong, not necessarily very culturally appropriate. The direct approach wasn't always the right one.

The fourth student I saw was very similar to the first three. We walked to the driftwood seat and we both sat facing the sea, which was just as good because this girl's beauty was distracting. Once we were settled in I said, "What's on you mind?"

As the others, she started right in on her story. "I wanted to talk to you about my brother."

"Go ahead," I encouraged her.

She proceeded to tell me a story about her brother, who was a few years older. He had gotten into drinking, which was an unfortunate problem among the youth – and older people – of the islands. I'm not sure if it was any worse than any other place; maybe in the small communities it was just more noticeable. What made the problem worse was that her father was a minister at a church in her village. She was from the island of Chuuk, which was about a thousand miles east of Palau. The brother's drinking was an embarrassment not only to her father but also to the whole family. There were times when the brother apologized for his drinking and said he wouldn't do it again. But he couldn't stay true to his word. The father had tried a number of things, but nothing seemed to help. She knew her brother had a problem, but she was also mad at him because she loved her father and hated to see her father suffer. It was a difficult situation, and there seemed to be no solution. The family couldn't disown the son, especially a minister. But until the son could get sober and stay that way it seemed the family was destined to suffer his sins.

She told her story with courage and candidness. She was very articulate, and I could hear the suffering in her voice.

I didn't know what to say. Advice seemed so clear when the other three girls spoke, and I felt comfortable trying to give them at least some direction. And they were thankful for what I had suggested to them.

This time I was at a loss. After she was finished and we sat for a while listening to the surf in the distance, I thinking furiously about what to say to her. I finally said, "Thanks for sharing your story. I know that was probably not easy." And I think that was true… it was not really the style of these island cultures to share feelings as we Americans are encouraged to do. I think my being an outsider made it feel safer for some of them. I then added, "But I have to be honest… I really don't know what to say. I don't think I can give you any advice in your situation."

"I don't want your advice," she said without hesitation, both chastising me as well as alleviating me of feeling I had to do something I couldn't.

She added, "I just wanted to tell my story… and for you to listen."

I nodded and we sat awhile in silence.

I said, "Thanks for telling me your story."

She said, "Thank you, too."

We walked back in silence. She said a quiet good-bye and went back to her school. The pick-up to take us back to the dock had arrived.

Of all the things I learned about teenagers in particular (and people in general) is that the first thing they want is to be listened to. I also found that in those situations where I think I am bringing something for people I instead get more in return. This was no exception. As a teacher I usually learn more from students than they learn from me. This was also true of my experience in Palau. The card I had in my pocket that allowed me entrance into Palau said, "Missionary," but it wasn't I who ministered to them as much as they ministered to me.

Remembering this story I also remembered how much Dad listened to me. I had a luxury that many teenagers don't have. I was lucky. I also felt lucky because I had a good friend that listened to me. I really missed Pilordes.

By this time of our trip on the *Suena* I felt a dearth of familiar stimuli, but more difficult, I felt a dearth of interaction with people, with friends, with life. One night we were sailing – slowly but smoothly. I was considering this during my night watch. It was very quiet, except for the sound of lapping water as we cut through the small waves, and it was also very dark – the moon had already set. I thought I heard something and saw movement at the front of the boat. I wondered, *Did a bird land?* I strained my eyes in the starlight, and among the dark shapes of sails, lines, mast, air ports, and other shadowy things. I thought I saw the silhouette of a booby. But in the limited light there were no definite outlines. I didn't move much and I tried to remain quite so as not to frighten it, if anything was there. Although I still couldn't see anything definite as I sat there, I could feel its presence. I began to trust my feeling that it was there and I was glad for the company.

A booby is a fairly large bird, about two and a half feet long, with a longer wingspan. They were named by sailors because of their seeming lack of intelligence for landing on ships and getting caught. It seems to me the lack isn't in the booby's intelligence, but in the lack of humans' friendliness; is it so hard for humans to return the friendly gestures nature makes to us?

After a few minutes I couldn't see any better, but I was sure it was a booby accompanying me on my watch. It was there for fifteen or twenty minutes before flying away. I was left with thoughts of the significance of quiet presence. With the dearth of stimuli I was able to be aware of another quiet presence I wouldn't have normally noticed. How much do I miss because of my own distractions? How much of the world, of life, do I miss because I'm not aware of the subtle things? It was as if something or someone was trying to tell me something through this experience. That there is more to the world than what meets the eye – or even what meets the mind! I was filled with a little needed hope, I knew there was more there around me, something always present that I may not be immediately aware of, but is present never-the-less. Working on my awareness was important to enrich my life of those subtle presences.

Although the voyage was difficult at times, I never regretted my experience. Because I was growing in new and unexpected ways I was happy for my experiences and I knew they were a benefit to me – more precious than I could imagine at that time. I knew that part of what I needed to learn was trust in God, trust in myself, and be more aware of all that is present to me, especially in ways I wouldn't normally recognize. As the trip went on I would have to learn more of these lessons. I also had time to review my life, consider what I had done and my impact on others, think about people who had influenced me, contemplate what mistakes I had made and what I hoped to do right, consider things I valued, things I wanted to value less, and things I wanted to value more. This desert experience was a way of removing all the usual everyday distractions that kept me from really looking at the person that I was, and hoped to be. In a way I had no choice but to look at who I was – what else could I do? There were no diversions from this. Not everything that I was seeing was pleasant, but without seeing those things there was no way that I could strive to improve myself, or at least be aware of those things, of who I really was on a deeper level.

I also found that I needed to look at things from different perspectives. For instance, compared to the Russian woman I had read about, on the *Suena* I was in paradise. I tried to appreciate that. Also, considering different time scales made a difference in how everything appeared; in relation to my life – or even a single year – this voyage was only a small piece. These realizations were a first step in changing my attitude. And at times life is just unpleasant. I find that when I acknowledge that life contains suffering, especially beyond my control, and accept it, the better off I am in coping with it. Sometimes flowing with it instead of struggling against it is a way to gain a certain amount of peace amidst the suffering. Find a deeper joy that that is not dependent on externals, but shines through even in the face of suffering.

But the desert wasn't all bad and agonizing. Some of my thoughts during this leg turned to Dad, who had died fourteen years earlier when I was a teenager. I remembered that we had dreams together. Dreams that we never had a chance to fulfill before he died of cancer. Some of our dreams were to travel to Hawaii together, go sailing together, learn to fly together. It wasn't until that leg, during the bleakest time of the desert experience, that I realized that I had fulfilled, or was fulfilling, at least two of these dreams. Although Dad wasn't there with me physically, I felt in a very real sense that he was sailing with me, similar to the feeling of knowing the booby was there even though I couldn't see it – that I wasn't sailing alone. It was still a difficult experience at times, but it had become special with a deeper meaning. I wasn't sailing alone any longer – Dad was sailing with me and my loneliness diminished. I was glad for the "desert" time to be able to realize this, and I wondered in what ways his spirit was present to help me be aware of this.

A number of years earlier a classmate and I were talking about the deaths of our fathers. She told me she had gone through a re-grieving process about eight years after the death of her father. Even though it had been a positive process for her, it was something I did not want to experience; I had grieved hard for about a year after Dad's death, and I didn't want to go through it again.

But just as my friend had talked about, I went through the same process. I was in Palau at the time and it was somewhat unexpected. It was also a different experience than I had expected. I thought it would be similar to the first time – dark and painful. But it wasn't. Mostly it was a time where I missed the fact that I could not share with Dad all the events that had happened in my life, like this sailing trip. Although I went through the re-grieving before sailing, sailing was something I would have loved to experienced with Dad, or at least talk to him about so he could at least share it vicariously with me. But that couldn't happen, and it needed to be grieved. It was also an acknowledgement of what he had given me; a strong work ethic, a sprit of adventure, an ability to see things with a positive attitude, compassion for others, and so much more. I was more mature, and far enough from the pain of his death that this re-grieving was, I think, more a completion of the original process that I was unable to complete that first year. I needed some time to pass, I needed to be more mature.

It was around this time that I read a piece by Dietrich Bonhoeffer that helped me to understand something I had, until that time, been unable to understand. That was a line of scripture that said, "Blessed are they who mourn, for they shall be comforted."* When I mourned Dad's death, I didn't feel comforted. Bonhoeffer's poem talked about the pain of separation of a lost loved one. In his poem he said he was not seeking to remove the pain, which was quite odd to me. But he went on to say the pain indicated there was still a connection, based on love. If we didn't love we wouldn't feel the pain. The pain was a result of the love. There was something that clicked in me and I finally understood.

I would always miss Dad, and the grieving process is not to eliminate that longing or pain. I still wanted to share my life with him face-to-face, in the flesh. But that longing, that pain, indicated that I still loved him, and I believe he still loved me. That pain of separation just meant that love is stronger than death and I will always have a connection with Dad.

A student of mine had lost her father while she was in high school, and it was a painful time for her. I had a copy of the Bonhoeffer poem on my desk, so I gave it to her, explaining what it meant to me. She did not say much, but I sensed a sort of sigh of relief in her demeanor. It did not eliminate her pain, but I think it gave her pain some meaning, which is vastly more important. Sometime later she thanked me, and then I knew it made a difference. I have since tried to find another copy of the Bonhoeffer poem, but I have been unable to re-locate one.

* Matthew 5:4

As my need for someone to talk to increased, I realized that Rick and Phyllis would be my only outlet for this need while I was still on the *Suena.* It was also apparent to me that I tended to be an introverted and closed person, not allowing others to know too much of what is in the depths of my being. But I also knew I didn't want to be too impenetrable. I was challenged to go to Rick and Phyllis, to be more connected to them, allow the chance for friendship. I had always been so strong, so male, so impermeable.

I hardly knew Rick and Phyllis, and Rick had the tendency to be so critical. But the pressure for making some sort of deeper connection with other human beings was building up.

It was the third day of the dog leg, during dinner, when I finally said, "Um ..."

Rick and Phyllis both looked at me. I tried to keep my voice from cracking as I said, "I'm not really used to this sailing business, as you know, and, um, I'm finding it kind of difficult adjusting to being on a sailboat for so long with a lack of familiar stimulation." Phyllis' expression showed understanding and compassion. Rick's face was stone. I felt awkward. I continued, "My worst time is during the day watch, so, um, I'm wondering if either of you have any suggestions to help me, ah, you know, keep myself occupied, and um, not be, ah, so lonely."

Phyllis continued to show sympathy, and a little bit of contempt slipped into Rick's expression. I said, "I think if I had someone to talk to for awhile during my day watch... that would help me out a lot. Even if it were only five or ten minutes. It would help to divert me, and it would be nice to get to know you two better."

"Well ..." Phyllis hesitated, "I usually get some sleep during that time, but I think I can spend some time at the end of my watch with you." Then she smiled and added, "My hobby is telling stories; I'll try some on you, and maybe you can tell me some, too."

"Sure," I said, feeling maybe my risk would be worth it.

Rick said, "Well, I understand that the sailing life takes a little getting used to, and there is a certain solitude to sailing which takes some adjusting to. I'll keep it in mind." I was encouraged by at least a little openness on Rick's part.

The main relief came with just sharing my struggle with Rick and Phyllis, and now there was also the hope that my day watch would be broken up with a little conversation.

True to her word, the next day Phyllis stayed above deck at the end of her watch to tell me some of her stories. I didn't have any clever stories to tell her, so I told her about Palau and other adventures I had had. Five minutes quickly became a half of an hour. I felt a little guilty that I had taken so much of her time, but I didn't feel any resentment in Phyllis. Rather, I felt she enjoyed the time, too. It was nice having someone to talk to, and it really did improve my spirits.

In the days that followed Phyllis made it a point to spend a few minutes after her watch talking to me, and to reciprocate I went on watch early, or spent a few minutes above deck with her after my breakfast to give back to her some conversation time, breaking up her watch, too. Usually, our donations of five minutes turned into fifteen or twenty. My day watches were still hard, but these conversations rose my spirits enough to make the days much more bearable. I got to know Phyllis much better and I'm sure she was able to see deeper into me. I also heard a number of good stories, and with Phyllis' encouragement I felt comfortable trying a few stories I'd heard here and there.

I found out we both missed trees being out on the water. That became our mantra throughout the remainder of the trip: Looking forward to enjoying the shade of a tree, its smell, the feel of its bark, and consciously appreciating it. We also played games of twenty questions, mini-mysteries, and other word games to pass the time and keep our minds occupied.

Rick wasn't much into conversations with me, and he never did come on watch early or spend time with me on my watch. However, Phyllis and I did get him into a few games of twenty questions and other word games at dinner time. It wasn't much, but that little extra interaction helped me to feel more comfortable with Rick and Phyllis, and I was especially thankful for the efforts by Phyllis to help keep me sane during my day watches. I felt much more connected to Phyllis, and I felt rewarded for taking a risk at opening up just a little. I also enjoyed the few times Rick participated. I enjoyed seeing him try to hold back his excitement when he had a "good one" for twenty questions.

It was the fourth day of the dog leg, and although Phyllis had spent some time talking to me at the beginning of my watch, by the end I was getting bummed again. I had only about fifteen minutes to go when Rick came from below deck and said, "Do you want to talk to a priest?"

My first thought was *Are we going to die?* The second thought was, *Maybe he sees how bummed I get on my watches and is sympathetic. But where, I wondered, is he going to get a priest, or is he just playing games with me?*

Rick saw my hesitation and added, "I got a priest on the radio from Pohnpei."

Although Micronesia covers an area about the size of the United States, the population could just about fit into a major league football stadium. My being associated with the Catholic Mission of Palau, I knew a number of the Priests in Micronesia, including Pohnpei. I had been to many of the Micronesia islands, including Pohnpei.

"What's his name?" I inquired.

"A guy named Father Cav."

"Cav!" I said, recognizing the name.

"I have him on the radio. Do you want to talk to him?"

"I'm on watch for another fifteen minutes," I said.

"That's okay," Rick said, "I'm on next; I'll cover you."

"Great!" I said and went below deck to talk on the radio.

It was a "small talk" conversation, but it was so good to hear a familiar voice. Granted, I didn't know Father Cav very well, but I had met him a few times and had eaten dinner at the same table with him on a number of occasions. In later years I was to get to know Farther Cav quite well, and he did me the honor of giving the sermon at my wedding many years later.

We talked for only a few minutes, but those few minutes lifted up my spirits. It was good to know that there were other humans still in the world, especially some who still remembered who I was. Before we signed off I asked him, as a favor, to try to contact Palau and say hello for me. I also asked him to tell those in Palau that I would be listening the same time the next day. He said he would relay the messages. Suddenly I didn't feel so lonely, and I was filled with hope again. I wondered why I hadn't utilized the radio earlier. I guess I figured I would not know any of the people on the other end.

It's amazing how these small events can have such great impact. I try to be more aware of these little things. It really is quite astonishing, when we are aware of them, how often the "little things" can grace our lives.

The whole trip we had used the engine far more than what we had expected. This leg was no different; we had had very little sailing time. And the weather had remained gloomy for days. Rick changed the engine oil approximately every seventy-five hours. He changed it just before we left Koror, and we had to change it twice during the trip (both times in rolling open ocean) and it was ready to be changed again when we finally arrived.

The fourth day of this leg, though, the wind had picked up and the seas were rougher. By evening the skies had become a steely grey. Rick listened to weather reports twice daily. He expected possible storms between New Guinea and Australia, but there had been none, nor were any forecast.

After dinner – no sunset, no drinks (we were out) – the dreary atmosphere made me want to escape in sleep. I went below deck after the dishes were completed and I laid down on the couch to read before I attempted sleep. Phyllis would be starting her watch soon.

I was about to put my book down (it was still trying to finish that dud of a book I had, and it was still going as slow as the trip was) when I heard Rick and Phyllis talking, or, rather, having one of their spats. I didn't think too much of it.

"Is it really that much of a problem?" I couldn't help but hearing Phyllis ask, upset.

"Yes," Rick said emphatically. "And it must be taken care of now."

"Can't it wait until morning when there's more light?" Phyllis pleaded.

"No, Phyllis!" Rick's voice was harsh.

"Rick!" Phyllis replied. It sounded like fear in her voice.

"Can you come up on deck?" Rick called to me.

"Sure," I said and jumped up and went up on deck to see what was up.

It wasn't what was up so much as what was down. Rick said, "The mainsail halyard came untied at the top, and we need to get it tied again. Now."

"But it's so dark now, and the seas are rough," Phyllis said. There definitely was fear in her voice. And she was right; the sun had already gone down and the seas were rougher than they had yet been. The swells were five to seven feet high and the *Suena* was rolling from side to side quite dramatically. I was surprised at the almost violent movement of the boat.

Rick was losing his patience with Phyllis and he very forcefully said – without anger, but with the authority of his experience – "Phyllis. We can't wait until morning. It will be dangerous to tie the mainsail halyard now under these conditions, but it would be more dangerous to wait until morning. Without the mainsail we are very unstable; look how we're rocking now! If the conditions get any worse, and there is a good chance they will, we will be in big trouble without a mainsail. The mainsail gives us our stability, and we need it, especially in these seas. We can't wait until morning!"

Phyllis didn't say anything more and Rick began to give instructions to us both.

I wondered why this had to happen at this time – after dark and in the roughest seas we had experienced so far. The one thing in our favor was that the moon was up – not full, but bright enough to give us a fair amount of light.

I lowered all the sails while Phyllis got out a hoisting plank and Rick put on his jacket. The plan was to attach the hoisting plank to the staysail halyard and use the hoisting plank as a seat for Rick. Phyllis and I would hoist Rick up the mast with the staysail halyard. Then I would hoist the mainsail halyard to Rick using the jib halyard. Once at the top, Rick would re-tie the mainsail halyard, then we would lower Rick and raise the mainsail and be on our way.

But it wasn't going to be easy. Phyllis and I would have to use pure muscle to raise Rick, and if we let go then Rick could very well fall to his death. Rick would also be among many ropes and cables which would compound the problem.

Soon everything was prepared to raise Rick up the mast. It was a tense moment. I could see fear in Phyllis' face and I could feel the adrenalin in my blood.

"Do everything exactly as I say," Rick advised. I could hear the tenseness in his voice, but it was devoid of any contempt, arrogance or anger that was so often there. "And respond – loudly – to all instructions."

"Okay," I responded. He didn't have to impress the import of the situation on me.

"Be careful, Rick," Phyllis pleaded. Rick didn't respond. Phyllis and I began to hoist Rick up the mast.

My thought was "This is real!" There was no practicing, and there was no second chance. We only had this one shot, and if we made a mistake it could be fatal. If there were any tests, this was it. Rick was hanging on a literal lifeline and he was depending on Phyllis and I to keep him from falling to his death. It was a strange feeling, and I was surprised how calm I was, yet I was far from cavalier about it. I also couldn't erase from my mind what would happen if Rick should fall. He would probably die, which would mean Phyllis and I would have to sail the *Suena* – for our lives – the rest of the way to Australia; we were too far to go back to Koror, and there were no other places nearer we could comfortably have gone at this point. Neither Phyllis nor I were experienced at sailing, and we had quite a distance of open ocean sailing to do, not to mention some tricky navigation through one more straight just before Darwin. Somehow, though, I knew we could do it, sail to Australia on our own if we had to – I had no doubt – but I didn't want the opportunity to find out.

When Rick was at the top of the mast, we wound the halyard line around the staysail winch for leverage. Phyllis cleated the line, but she held on for extra safety. While Phyllis was doing this I was attaching the mainsail halyard to the jib halyard, to hoist up to Rick. Rick yelling instructions; I responded to each one. I was full of adrenalin, but my mind was clear and I was able to do what I needed to do. The biggest worry was to be sure the lines didn't get tangled, which was tricky, and could have been dangerous.

Finally I got everything arranged and hoisted the mainsail halyard up to Rick, who was swaying fiercely at the top of the mast. Because he was at the top of the mast, he experienced the greatest amount of movement. I admired him for his composure, knowledge and strength.

Once Rick had the mainsail halyard in hand we could do nothing more but wait for Rick to do his stuff. Phyllis and I didn't have anything to say. I looked around and couldn't help but to notice that the sea was beautiful in the moon light, and the swells were very large. When I looked up at Rick working at the top of the mast it was an eerie sight. The top of the mast being so far from the pivot point of the rocking boat meant that for every roll of the boat he etched a huge arc. He moved a long distance in a short time, so he must have been experiencing excessive forces. When the boat rocked to one side Rick was hanging far out over the water, then in a matter of seconds he would swing and be far out over the water on the other side. I could hardly imagine what it must have been like for Rick; it must have taken a lot of strength to hold on, not to mention courage.

After an extremely long five minutes Rick yelled down that he was finished. I felt a wave of relief rush over me, but it wasn't over yet; we still had to lower Rick safely. But with no hitches, in another couple of minutes Rick was safely back on deck and we were all able to breath sighs of relief, but it was a number of minutes before I was able to breath normally again. We raised the mainsail, stabilized the boat, raised the jib and staysail and we were sailing again. I was free to catch some zees, but now I had too much adrenalin in my system to sleep. Sailing really could be exciting, and these times helped to dissipate the times of idleness.

❁

We had some wind the last few days of the first part of the dog leg, but the wind was beating against us, so we had to tack, which made our going very slow. At least we were sailing. The five days – not the three I had hoped for – it took us to get to the point where we turned south toward Darwin seemed like an eternity; Helen's Reef seemed like years before. We had, however, made progress, even though it was slow.

We were now beginning to head south! I was getting anxious to get to Darwin, but I knew we still had about three to five days on the water. And the biggest chance to hit a storm was in this last section.

Rick usually told Phyllis and I what the weather reports were, not so much as a matter of routine, but more as a conversation piece at dinner – every little news item is something to talk about when your world is 36 feet long, occupied by only two other people. This dinner he said, "The weather will be okay for a day or so, but there is a high pressure cell building northwest of Australia. We could get some winds from that. Maybe fifteen or twenty knots."

"Is fifteen or twenty knots a lot?" I asked.

He chuckled a little and said, "Fifteen or twenty knots are quite stiff winds."

"Then they will help to sail faster," I said with little conviction, hoping I would be right, but knew I was wrong.

Rick confirmed my intuitions by saying, "Twenty knots is too strong of a wind to really sail in, unless the conditions are just right. We might be able to sail in fifteen, but we won't know until it happens and we know the situation. It all depends on so much: the swells, the waves, the precipitation …"

"Is the high pressure cell heading this way?"

"It is hard to tell at this point, but it doesn't look good. I would predict that we are going to feel some of it, at least with strong winds in a day or two. But, then again, maybe not."

So we began the last section of open ocean. I could almost see the light at the end of the tunnel, but not quite yet. My hope of being so close was dampened by the prospect of heavy winds, rough seas, and possible storms. I tried to keep an attitude of "more excitement" rather than of "possible danger."

Thus we began the second half of the dog-leg.

Chapter 6

Arriving in Darwin

It was a beautiful day, and it sure felt good to see the sun after a number of days of overcast skies. It also felt better that we were on the final leg – a few more days and we would be in Darwin. The sky was mostly clear with only a few non-threatening clouds brushed into the blue. We could see Kepulauan Aru in the far distance off the port beam and Kepulauan Kai closer off the starboard beam. The only thing we could have used more of was wind – it was very light – but at least we were sailing. My spirits were still down, surprisingly, but lifted more than the previous few days. I looked forward to the end of my day watch, not so much that it would be over as much as I was hoping I would be able to talk to someone from Palau on the radio.

Sure enough, when the appointed time came there was a person from Palau on the radio. It wasn't the person I really wanted to talk to, but it was someone I knew. Not really a friend, but an acquaintance whose son lived in Sydney, Australia. After arriving in Darwin I would make myself to Sydney from where I would fly back to Colorado. I hoped to stay in Sydney at lease a few days to kick around, and now I had a place to stay. He said everything was set, no worries. He also promised to deliver some messages for me to my friends in Palau. A slight let down, but it felt good to have talked to someone from Palau.

By evening we were using the engine again. If we were going to get any wind from the building weather systems, we sure hadn't gotten it yet. At sunset – the first beautiful one in many days – there were some clouds to the south that put some butterflies in my stomach. They turned out to be nothing.

The weather reports continued to forecast heavy weather to the northeast of Australia. Rick thought we would get high winds from that weather system, but so far we were still using the engine, puttering along at a very slow pace. We had used the engine so much already that we began to wonder if we would have enough fuel to get us to Australia. We needed some wind. But we didn't need any gales.

Finally on the second day on this last straight shot to Australia we were sailing at about three knots. It felt agonizingly slow, and Phyllis said, "Why don't we use the engine?"

Rick replied, irritated, "Why not sail? We aren't in a hurry, are we?"

"But Rick," Phyllis protested, "we're only going three knots. Already it's taken a lot longer than we thought."

"We'll get there," Rick insisted.

"Rick!" Phyllis said, frustrated.

"Phyllis," Rick said with irritation, "with out any fuel we won't get there either. I'd like to have some fuel for the last straight into Darwin."

"Rick, we'll be careful to save some."

Rick grumbled some more, but the engine was soon started, which gave us about five knots with the sails. I was glad to be traveling at more than three knots – I felt Phyllis was arguing as much for me as she was for herself – but I found myself wishing I could relax and enjoy sailing at only three knots.

The day watches continued to be dry, but Phyllis continued to play word games with me, and we continued to exchange stories. I also finally gave up the book I was plodding through and picked up a Tony Hillerman book that both Phyllis and Rick recommended. It was the first Tony Hillerman book I read, and was definitely not the last. Reading a good book can make such a big difference on one's outlook in a dry situation. It was stimulating in a good way, was a good escape, and it took place not far from my home which gave me a sense of the familiar and of home. It was like being home early.

It wasn't until that second night that we finally got some wind. It was during Phyllis' watch that she and Rick put up the sails – I was peacefully sleeping at the time. The seas were quite large and slightly rough. Talk about a pitching boat! The front of the sailboat would pitch up to a thirty degree angle, then down the same amount. Often when it pitched down the prow would dip into the water, then when it pitched up again it would throw a huge splash of water and spray into the air. Also, every time the boat pitched down it would make a strange gushing and banging sound. The big waves were really loud, and it echoed inside the cabin – part of the nature of a steel sailboat.

It took me awhile to get used to this new movement and sounds of the *Suena*. We were, finally, sailing at quite a clip. Because the winds had picked up quite a bit,

Rick and I put up the small jib. Actually, I put up the small jib, everything from getting it out of the rear storage compartment, taking off the big jib and storing it, hanking on the small jib, raising it, to adjusting its trim. Rick talked me through the parts I needed help on. I did all the work, but I was thankful for the action. It was part of sailing, which I had come to do, and the pitching sailboat made it that much more fun! I was a happy person again.

I think it was probably a good thing that my first watch in this new weather was at night. I trusted the night, so I wasn't quite so concerned about the large waves, and pitching boat. The waves were even larger than the mainsail-halyard incident days earlier.

At the beginning of my watch I was given the same bearing instructions as usual, plus I was advised to clip into the safety line. I wore Rick's raincoat for warmth, which easily clipped into the safety line. I was also told that if the speed got above seven knots that I should call Rick so we could reef the mainsail if needed.

The more aggressive movement of the *Suena* was different, but soon I loved it. This was sailing! It was like riding a huge bronco with the pitching motion. It was one of my best nights on watch. I sat on the deck instead of in the cockpit (with the safety line this time), and I just enjoyed the ride. Occasionally I would get splashed wildly with a wash of water, but with the raincoat I stayed relatively dry and warm. It's such an incredible experience to be sailing instead of using the engine. I fell in love with the trip again. And sailing, as always, was great. I loved checking the trim, keeping on course, studying the horizon, raising and lowering sails. I realized that if we had sailed like this the whole trip I would have loved every minute and would not have had any problems with being bummed out, even if the trip took as long as it did. There is no substitute for sailing, real sailing.

We were sailing at a little more than seven knots – I loved finally traveling at a decent clip – and the ride was wildly fun. I should have called Rick because we were over seven knots, but everything seemed to be going just fine, so I didn't bother.

The next day we sailed, although at a slower pace, but we were sailing, which made even the day watch enjoyable. It was amazing how just sailing instead of motoring made such a difference.

The next night was the same as the previous; fast and aggressive. Again I used the safety lines and Rick's coat. I sat on the deck and relished the movement of the boat. A lot of wind, a lot of spray, a slight chill in the air, and the boat rising and falling. I could feel the strength of the motion which just reinforced my respect for nature. I could feel there was danger involved, but over all it was an exhilarating experience. This was the highlight of my experience and I soaked up every moment sitting there on the *Suena*'s deck.

The next evening the winds were slight, but there was a real possibility that they might pick up – There was still a forecast of heavy winds to the southeast moving toward us. We had the small jib still up. Rick said he wanted to put up the large jib in the light winds and have Phyllis or me call him if the winds picked up appreciably, so he could help me put up the small jib again and, if needed, reef the mainsail. I didn't agree, but who was I to say since I had virtually no sailing experience? But I said so anyway!

"Rick, don't you think it would be better to just leave the small jib up since we expect stronger winds later? It would save us the trouble of changing a sail twice, plus it will save you from getting up, and me from having to make that decision. We can leave up the staysail to compensate for the small jib, and if the winds really pick up then I can lower the staysail myself – without having to wake you up."

Rick just couldn't agree with me. I tried my best to be as tactful as possible, being really careful that my tone of voice was meek. But Rick couldn't admit outright that I was correct, that I had learned something about sailing, and learned quite well. He said his idea was better, and he proceeded to explain why.

We discussed the matter for about five minutes. I realized pretty quick that I couldn't press my point, and I was ready to follow whatever instructions he gave me. I tried to see things from his point of view and use it as a learning experience. I was resigned to just do it his way.

By the end of our discussion, however, he said, "So we'll leave the small jib up with the staysail, and if the wind picks up a lot you can lower the staysail yourself. If, however, it gets real windy then you can call me to reef the main."

"Sounds like a good plan to me," I responded.

As it turned out, the wind did pick up quite a bit, and it was a repeat of the night before. Again, I loved the bronc ride, and we got past seven knots. It felt good to make decisions and adjustments on my own without having to call Rick for help.

It was a great few days of sailing. The only problem – if it really was a problem – was that when I was sleeping I would occasionally wake up, the *Suena* pitching quite a bit, crashing into the hull with loud booms. The vehemence of the pitching and the loudness of the booms made the situation seem serious, especially when I would fitfully wake from a sleep. From below everything seemed much worse, and half asleep my mind didn't always work perfectly. I would think to myself, *What did I get myself into? I'm on a thirty-six foot piece of tin being thrown around in the middle of a raging ocean like a toy boat! Is it sane for people to tempt nature like this?* It was a strange feeling, but I would fall right back to sleep again.

In those brief moments I could palpably feel the vastness of the ocean and the tiny-ness of the *Suena* in comparison. I felt a sort of on-my-own feeling, in the middle of the ocean, disconnected from the rest of the world. There would be no help if needed. We take for granted emergency rooms and such, but being far from these things I could feel a sense of disconnect, an aloneness.

I felt a similar feeling when Dad died. Suddenly I was on my own. And although I knew it to some extent at the time (which became more apparent as time passed) that Dad had equipped me with the tools and know-how to survive on my own, it was as if Dad had taught me how to sail life and he gave me the tools to navigate the world and manage the storms. I felt sometimes like I was on my own, but I really wasn't. Dad gave me a seaworthy boat capable to manage the storms, and the knowledge to captain my own journey. I realized I was now a sailor in more ways than one.

The days of this last leg were fine as long as we were sailing, but there were still, surprisingly, times when we had to use the engine. We were close enough to Australia by this time that during these engine times I had hope enough to keep from slipping into despair. There was still "weather" building over the northeast of Australia – keeping butterflies in my stomach – but no dangerously high winds yet, and the skies continued to be beautiful with only a few clouds to spot the blue.

The next day Phyllis called me up during her watch to see a number of dolphins paralleling the *Suena*. It was nice to have more companions, although they didn't stay long, maybe ten minutes.

Their presence seemed to say, "Welcome to Australia!"

It was nice to have their company. Something about dolphins is very comforting to me. They have a spiritual feeling to me, and it is nice to know that there are beings in the world that seem to be peaceful and intelligent. It is sad to me that they were once hunted for their valuable oil – a small amount at that – that was extracted from their heads. The oil was used to lubricate delicate watch mechanisms. If people only knew. If they knew their watch was oiled at the expense of a dolphin's life. If they could have experienced these graceful, peaceful and powerful beings would they still have bought the watch knowing it was at the expense of one of these creatures? I would like to believe in the capacity of compassion in people. But sometimes I have to wonder. After all, there were those who saw the majesty of the buffalo, yet still chose to shoot them. How much easier it is to lack compassion and empathy in a disconnected world. For me it is important to try to stay connected to some extent, and experiencing those dolphins was a moment of connection for me. In what other ways do innocent creatures, like the dolphin, suffer because of our ignorance and disconnect?

I just enjoyed having the dolphins swim alongside us. I felt honored by their presence. I tried to count them, but they popped up for only a second at a time then would stay under for a minute or more; I couldn't know where they would come up next. I surmised, however, that it was a family of three or four.

Each day I could see from the daily markings Rick made on the charts that we were in fact getting closer and closer to Australia. We were about a day out, and the weather reports were getting worse and worse – they were predicting gale force winds along the coasts of Australia, moving in our direction from the southeast. However, where we were it was as calm and smooth as could be. In fact, we were using the engine because of lack of wind. I figured we would get to the coast and experience the ride of our life. But that wasn't to be either.

I woke up one morning and land was in sight. It was such a glorious sight to me; it was Australia! We had one more straight to navigate, but for all practical purposes we were there.

Rick was studying the charts and tide tables closely. We would do about half the straight that first day, and then we would have to anchor for the night and wait for the right tides for the tricky second half. Apparently the tides at Darwin were some of the strongest in the world, and had to be timed with care.

During my day watch all three of us were above deck while I navigated as Rick instructed. The weather was sunny and calm, but we were still waiting for the wind. We puttered along, slowly, but I didn't mind so much any more; we had made it.

We entered the straight. It was wide at the entrance, but now land was on either side of us again. We followed it and it became narrower and the term "straight" fit. Just after my watch we anchored – retrieving the anchor from stowage – in a fairly narrow section of the straight. We did our best to position the *Suena* out of the lane of traffic. We had dinner together. No one was on watch and no one had to go on watch since we were no longer moving. The lifting of watch responsibility felt good.

But Rick was nervous. He was nervous about hitting the tides just right, and he was nervous about the straight. He said it would be a tricky one. I guess I had a different way of looking at it. I figured that if it was a well used straight and there was a lot of commercial and recreational traffic through the straight every day, which there was, then it should be well marked and easily passable. Also, this was Australia so it was sure to be marked with stricter standards than Indonesia, and the charts were probably more trustworthy. We seemed to be on pretty solid ground here.

Rick told us that we would have to leave early and that we all had to be on deck for the passage.

Of course, I thought, why would I miss it?

After dark we could see the lights of another sailboat about the same size as the *Suena* anchored about a hundred yards behind us. Rick was able to get them on the radio. They were also waiting for the morning tide to go into Darwin. They had navigated this straight before. After Rick got off the radio I asked him, "Why don't you just follow him through? They've been through it and maybe they can help out."

He answered angrily, "If I follow them I could very well follow them into danger. I have my own charts and I can navigate it myself. I can't trust another sailboat."

I didn't say anything else. I knew Rick was impervious to suggestions on this point.

Rick and Phyllis went to bed fairly early. I stayed up a little while longer; I couldn't sleep. The sky was so beautifully clear and full of shimmering stars, and being in the southern hemisphere the constellations were unfamiliar to me. I was enjoying the stars I had never seen before. Plus I was basking in the feeling that we had arrived – almost, anyway. What a great feeling it was. I was finally in Australia! I had a feeling of accomplishment, even though it was not completely over. I was practically on the other side of the world, which the stars attested to.

The next morning the alarm woke us all – the first time it was used on the whole trip. It was still dark out, but the eastern horizon was beginning to glow. I had enough time for a very quick bite to eat, but I had to be up on deck for our departure – no delaying. As I raised the anchor I could see that the current from the tide was indeed strong – it was flowing like a river – and we had to go with it. There was enough of a wind, and in the right direction, to easily sail with. Soon we were under way.

There were too many clouds to make a good sunrise, but otherwise it seemed like the beginning of a good day. We were moving at a good clip and everything was smooth. Rick was at the prow with his hand-held compass and maps, navigating. Phyllis was at the tiller taking Rick's directions. I, basically, had no real job but to be handy. Occasionally Rick instructed me to count how many times a light blinked on a light house, but other than that I watched the many birds through the binoculars or studied the trees on the shore.

The other sailboat anchored near us the night before was also making the passage about the same time as we were; they were a few hundred yards behind us. Slowly they were gaining on us. One, then another, shrimp boat passed us going in the other direction, going out to sea. It wasn't long before the other sailboat passed us up. I was jealous at their speed and ease, and I was convinced that Rick was just being too cautious. I wanted to suggest to Rick to just pull in behind them and follow them in, but I knew better not to. Rick was showing all his signs of being tense, especially with his short, curt commands and replies. He had been busy taking sightings with his compass.

In the absence of conversation I casually made the observation, "The lights on that light house behind us are now a different color."

Rick snapped at me, "When did they change?"

"About a minute ago," I estimated.

"Why didn't you tell me?" he demanded.

"I didn't know I was supposed to," I said.

"You must tell me everything!"

I didn't know what to say.

He added, "Everything is important and I must know!"

Maybe if I had more sailing experience I could have better appreciated the passage through that last straight, but as I perceived it, it seemed like a wide, deep, well marked passage. The evidence was the sailboat that whizzed passed us and was now a quarter-mile ahead of us. But I complied with Rick and let him know everything I saw that I deemed important: I pointed out all the lighthouses I saw, the colors of their lights, how often they blinked, any other boats I saw, changes in wind direction – anything. This kept him quiet; he neither thanked me, but nor did he scold me. I also noticed the land, the trees, the birds, the sky, the waters. It was a good exercise in awareness of my surroundings.

It only took us about two hours to finish the narrow part of the passage, then we were in the Darwin Bay. We were basically free, no more tricky navigation, we could relax the rest of the way in. In the distance, miles away, Darwin could just be made out with the binoculars. It was an exciting feeling to see Darwin! And the day was looking better. The sun was out, the waters were smooth, and we had a brisk wind in a good direction. I'm not sure we could have asked for a better final day. We had made our destination, we were alive and well, and the weather was cooperating.

Slowly Darwin became more distinct as we got closer. The sun was strong and bright, but the brisk wind kept the day cool. There were a number of boats – many sailboats – out in the bay; I could feel in the air that we were approaching a metropolitan area. I was getting excited, but we still had hours to go. It always seems like that last little bit after a long journey is the longest and slowest, but at least the day was nice and we were sailing. I could see the solid land I would be standing on by the end of the day.

I had no more responsibilities above deck, so I went below deck and tried to read. I was on my second Tony Hillerman book – another good book – but this day even Tony Hillerman couldn't distract me from the excitement I was feeling to be on land again. I had to find something to keep myself busy, so I packed up my stuff – three times! Unfortunately packing took me only ten minutes; I really didn't have that much stuff. In the end I found myself again above deck, binoculars in hand, studying Darwin's seaside, dreaming about that first shower I would take, the long walk afterward, then winding down the night by watching television in bed.

I sensed that Rick and Phyllis were tense and nervous. They were more snappy with each other than usual, and there just seemed to be a tension in the air. Rick didn't have much to say to me (as was the case throughout the trip) but his instructions to me had a harsh tone, despite the fact there wasn't a tense situation at hand. Rick asked me to begin preparing the boat for immigration – the immigration officers would come to the *Suena* once we were in Darwin to search the boat. To make it easier and faster (they charged by the amount of time it took to complete the job) we put all canned goods in one storage area, cereals and grains in a different location, leftover vegetables and fruits in yet a different place. Other parts of the sailboat were readied for our entry into Darwin. This kept me busy for a short while.

By the time Darwin could be seen clearly everything was prepared. Boat traffic was getting thicker which required more attention on Rick's part. The wind had also picked up – finally feeling the effects of the weather we heard about on the radio and the waters were becoming rougher. The sun was still intense. No one spoke much. I took a few pictures, and I had Phyllis take a picture of me near the mast, bandana wrapped on my head, my tan (as good as it gets), and nineteen days of facial hair growth.

As we got closer I got more excited to feel solid ground under my feet, Rick got more harsh with me and more critical of Phyllis, and Phyllis became more whiny in response to Rick's barbs. I could tell that Rick and Phyllis had some unresolved business regarding their parting in Darwin, and the tension was thick on the *Suena*.

He said to me, as a captain, "After a long passage like we have just completed the ship needs to be cleaned thoroughly, especially the kitchen area. There's a scrubber under the sink in the container on the left side, and some cleanser, too. Use that to clean the counter and walls in the kitchen area. Get all that grime and scum. Then do over by the map room."

I was on the trip to crew, so I felt that when I'm told to do work then I do it. I didn't complain or ask questions. I wasn't in the mood to scrub, but it was part of my job, and I also knew it would keep me occupied.

I went below deck to begin my work and I heard Phyllis protest to Rick, "Why are you making him do that? We're almost there; you and I can do that tomorrow or the next day."

Rick scolded Phyllis, "He needs to do his part, Phyllis. He's hardly done anything this whole trip."

"What are you talking about, Rick?" Phyllis said with a mixture of surprise and anger.

Rick insisted, "He needs to do his part!"

They continued their argument in hushed tones.

I got the feeling Rick meant for me to hear what he said.

I was both surprised and hurt. I questioned myself, *Was I not holding up my end of the bargain? Was there more I was supposed be doing that I didn't know about? Did I ever refuse work? Was I being a lazy-ass this whole trip? Why didn't he tell me to do more? I would have done it.* Feeling I hadn't performed my duty bothered me, especially when the implication was that I didn't pull my weight. But this time it didn't take me long to convince myself that I had done everything that I had been told I was expected to do, and I had done it well. Phyllis' objections to Rick helped to confirm this for me.

When I was finished scrubbing, Rick looked at my work and said, "Can't you get the grime better than that?" I wanted to shout back, "You should have seen it before I started to scrub!" But instead I just put more cleanser on the scrubpad and continued to work it.

It was about four in the afternoon and we were about a quarter-mile from shore in the midst of much boat traffic: sailboats, motorboats, small ships, large ships. It felt good to be in the activity of a city again. Phyllis steered while Rick examined the map for the tie-up point – Rick had talked to immigration earlier on the radio, and they had given him a tie-up location. The water was quite rough; there was a stiff wind, with occasional strong gusts. Rick would look up occasionally to criticize or scold Phyllis for her steering. The tension seemed to be even thicker, almost volatile; I was glad that I would be off the boat in a short while, possibly within the hour.

We found where we were supposed to wait for the immigration team and headed in that direction. Unfortunately, it happened to be in the middle of a small Sunday afternoon sailing regatta. Rick and Phyllis argued as to whether they should cut through the race or anchor someplace nearby. Rick insisted we cut through the race and wait for the immigration officers where he was instructed.

The captain spoke, so we did such.

We came fairly close to colliding with another boat. Rick ignored the Australian-accented profanity as we moved to the center of the circling boats; I could see embarrassment on Phyllis' face.

When the immigration officers arrived I was bursting with excitement. I hoped to get a ride with them back to shore, escape the tension; I had all my things ready. It was a beautiful afternoon with the sun sparkling on the water, sailboats cruising in the stiff winds, motorboats flitting in and out of traffic. We were anchored only a couple of hundred yards from shore, from the heart of downtown Darwin. We happened to arrive on Queen's Day, and there was a large celebration in the city. Up on the hill we could see crowds of people milling around under banners and amidst booths, the sounds of bands giving the atmosphere a festive flavor, and even a whiff of barbeque reached us on the occasional gust.

The three immigration officers boarded the *Suena.* They were very friendly folk and their Australian accents were fascinating. It was so nice to have other people on board to talk with and interact with. Their presence dismantled all the tension that was present between Rick and Phyllis, at least for the time being.

They were on the *Suena* just over a half an hour, inspecting all the holds, going over Rick's travel logs and stamping our passports They welcomed us to Australia and left with smiles. Unfortunately, they couldn't take me with them because of regulations. I hated to see them go, but I knew I would still be off the *Suena* before dark.

It was almost two hours later that I finally set foot on shore. We had to motor the *Suena* up and around a point to a marina. The currents and winds were against us, and the engine seemed extra sluggish. When we reached the marina Rick was having fits because it was so shallow, and he couldn't decide on a place to anchor. Finally, with no choice, we anchored in the best spot available.

I helped prepare the *Suena* for the night. It had to be well secured against thieves for we were back in "civilization," and neither Rick nor Phyllis would spend the night on the boat that night. We took down the staysail and jib and stowed them. The mainsail was lowered and secured. Ropes were wound and stowed, along with other things. Equipment was locked tight. The dingy was pumped up, the floor put in and the engine bolted on.

Then it was time to go. Rick was in the dingy getting the engine started. Phyllis would stay on the *Suena* finishing up while Rick ferried me to shore. I would meet them the next day, the last time before we all went our separate ways. Phyllis handed me a piece of blue paper – it was an Australian ten dollar bill.

"You'll need this until you can exchange some more money." She gave me a smile and a hug. I climbed down into the dingy and Phyllis handed me down my last bag. Rick gunned the motor as soon as I was seated and we headed for the pier.

It was about a hundred yards in rough water. I didn't want to get wet, but the waves and wind made sure I got wet and cold. To my surprise, Rick was unusually friendly on that very last leg.

He said, "I hope you had a good time. It was nice to have you along."

"I enjoyed it," I said.

He hesitated before saying, "I hope Phyllis and I didn't dampen the mood any." He paused then explained, "It was our last passage together and we were dealing with that."

I wanted to yell back at him, "The problem was that you were not dealing with your separation!" But I kept quiet.

He added, "And she can get so uptight sometimes. I've traveled with women before, but they've always been more relaxed then Phyllis."

He didn't say anything more, and there was just the buzz of the motor and the hiss of the wind. I wanted to add "You're the one who was so uptight, not Phyllis!" But we were only twenty yards from shore and there was no point getting into it.

I said, "How much money do I owe you for my part of the food and gas?"

He calculated verbally all the expenses and quoted me a cost. It was lower than I had expected – my impression was that he was trying to make up for his harshness. I accepted his offer.

We arrived at the steps leading up to the pier. I gave him the agreed upon money from my wallet, loaded my bags on my person, and mounted the steps.

"Bye," we both said to each other and went in our different directions.

Chapter 7

Epilogue

After leaving the *Suena* I just wanted to get to a motel, take a long shower, watch some television and sleep on a real bed. When I climbed the latter up to the top of the pier, I saw that I had to walk about 100 yards to some buildings, where I hoped was a phone I could call the motel that had been recommended to me by a friend in Palau. I had already made reservations, I just needed to get there.

The hundred yards seemed like a long walk, especially with my three bags. Phyllis had given me ten Australian dollars, which I changed at the seedy store at the end of the pier and used the phone to call a cab. I described as best I could where I was. They said they would send a cab as soon as one was available – all were busy at the moment. The store was not a place that seemed welcoming, so I sat outside on a bench waiting for the cab. The hour that I waited seemed like an eternity as I longed for a shower and a bed.

The cab came and on the way to the motel I felt better already. The motel was a simple, but very clean and a friendly establishment. It was run by a young couple with a small child, who were very friendly. It was almost as if we had been long lost friends, and I felt very at home. I was soon in a clean room with a large bed and television. It felt great to put my bags down, lay on the bed and turn on the television. I lay on the bed for a few minutes soaking in the roominess, the space that was all to myself, with the thought that I could actually go for a walk. But a shower – a real shower – was in order, and it was time. It is amazing how the right perspective can put into focus the preciousness of an everyday activity, such as a shower.

I got a nice stream of warm water going then stepped in and enjoyed a nice long shower. What a pleasure! I enjoyed the water flowing over me for probably twenty minutes. I wanted to stay longer, but I knew more showers would come soon, so I pulled myself away.

I considered letting my beard and mustache grow since I had more of a head start than I ever had, but even after almost three weeks I still didn't have much. Plus it just itched, so it had to go. It took awhile to get it all, but as it slowly came off I began to feel lighter and fresh. It was a wonderful transformation.

After I had finished shaving, I stood in the restroom looking in the mirror, and I saw an amazing thing. I saw Dad's face staring back at me. No, I was not seeing visions, but I could the features of Dad in my own face. Of course this would be expected, being of the same genetic line, but I hadn't thought of it this way before – Dad's features in my face. It was a realization that Dad was with me in yet one more way. Dad had been with me during the entire journey, and he would be with me the rest of my life. But not only would he be with me in my features, he would always be with me in all that he taught me and in how he helped me perceive the world. And, no less important, he would be with me in spirit, and our bond of love will always be real. I was just beginning to understand how strong these connections really were, and how much impact Dad had – and still has – on my life.

After showering and shaving it was time for a walk. It was early evening, so there was still quite a bit of time for a nice walk. I left the motel room and wandered randomly – it was nice to have no particular goal in mind. Walking, I began to think of Pilordes. I really did miss her, and I longed to share with her these wonderful moments and thoughts I had.

That night I watched television, which I had been looking forward to. But, I discovered very soon, just as before the trip, there still wasn't much worth watching. So I made it an early evening and went to bed. The large, unmoving bed, was wonderful. I fell asleep with a smile on my face.

I woke up about 2:00 in the morning and my first thought was, It's past midnight, I should be on watch! I had a moment of panic. Then I realized that I was in a motel and didn't have watch duty, which should have been a relief, but I was still half asleep. It took a while for me to accept the thought that I was no longer on the *Suena*. Part of the reason for this was that the room was rolling from side to side and pitching back and forth – just like the *Suena* at sea. I got out of bed and stumbled to the window. I opened the curtain, and when I saw solid land the feeling of being out to sea subsided. I looked for a few moments, feeling the solid ground beneath me, then I went back to bed.

The same thing happened the next night. It took my body and mind some time to transition from the sailing experience back to being a land-lubber.

I stayed at the motel for two days just relaxing, taking a lot of walks, going into town for coffee, enjoying warm showers, and just generally enjoying some "down time." I met Rick and Phyllis one more time and we saw a movie and ate dinner at a sailing friend of Rick's. It was a pleasant time and it allowed us one last time together without tension, so the final parting was under good terms, which was nice.

After my stay in Darwin I took a bus to Sydney. On the way I stopped in Alice Springs for two days, Aldelaide for most of one day, then on to Sydney. There I stayed in Sydney for four days with the family of a friend from Palau. By pleasant accident I ran into some other friends from Palau – what were the odds of that? – and we spent some time together. I even visited a former student who was attending college in Sydney. It was a very pleasant time and a wonderful conclusion to my adventure.

But it was also time to go home. Nine days after setting foot in Darwin, Australia I boarded a plane and flew fourteen hours back to the mainland. Eventually I ended up in Colorado, where I had grown up.

But the pull of the islands was too strong and in a few months I was back in the islands for many more years. I was able to reconnect with my "friend" Pilordes. As mentioned earlier, we did marry, although I had to wait eight years. It was worth it.

I grew up in Colorado, but I feel more at home in the islands. I have visited Palau since, and the roots I had set there during those six year were still in place. It was a reassuring feeling. I hope one day to return to, and live, in Micronesia. And I look forward to showing my son, Richard – named after Dad – an important piece of my heart.

About the Author

Tyler Rush Bangert grew up in the mountains of Colorado, where he lived until he was 18. He got a degree in Aerospace Engineering from Saint Louis University. Before going into engineering, however, he first spent a year as a full-time volunteer in a shelter for homeless women in New Orleans.

He then worked as an Aerospace Engineer in Houston, Texas with MacDonnell Douglas Corporation in the Space Shuttle program. With adventure still in his soul, however, he began to take courses in education and began teaching.

He soon found himself teaching at Mindszenty High School in the Republic of Palau. He spent six years in Palau in the western Pacific before returning to the US mainland to finish a Master's degree.

After two years he returned to the western Pacific, but this time to the island of Saipan of the Northern Marianas Islands. He taught at Mount Carmel School for one year before becoming principal for the high school, where he served for five more years. While there he married the love of his life, Pilordes.

They returned to the mainland and have spent the last six years in Arizona with their son Richard. He currently serves as principal of Seven Mile Elementary School on the White Mountain Apache Tribe reservation.

His passions include: his family, drumming, reading, writing, games, education and enjoying life.

Printed in the United Kingdom
by Lightning Source UK Ltd.
136056UK00001B/392/P

9 781438 914947